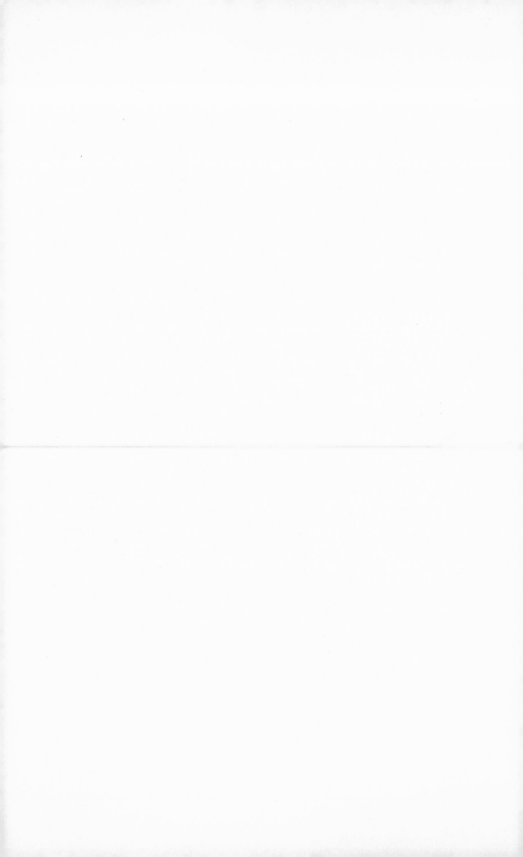

HEALING PRAYER

HEALING PRAYER

GOD'S DIVINE INTERVENTION
IN MEDICINE, FAITH,
AND PRAYER

REGINALD CHERRY, M.D.

CARMEL • NEW YORK 10512

www.guideposts.org

This Guideposts edition is published by special arrangement with Thomas Nelson Publishers.

Scripture quotations noted AMPLIFIED are from THE AMPLIFIED BIBLE: Old Testament. Copyright © 1962, 1964 by Zondervan Publishing House (used by permission); and from THE AMPLIFIED NEW TESTAMENT. Copyright © 1958 by the Lockman Foundation (used by permission).

Scripture quotations noted NIV are from THE HOLY BIBLE: NEW INTERNATIONAL VERSION®. Copyright © 1973, 1978, 1984 by International Bible Society. Used by permission of Zondervan Publishing House. All rights reserved.

Scripture quotations noted TLB are from *The Living Bible*, copyright © 1971. Used by permission of Tyndale House Publishers, Inc., Wheaton, Illinois 60189. All rights reserved.

Scripture quotations noted NKJV are from THE NEW KING JAMES VERSION. Copyright © 1979, 1980, 1982, Thomas Nelson, Inc., Publishers.

Scripture quotations noted KJV are from the KING JAMES VERSION.

Scripture quotations noted NCV are from The Everyday Bible, New Century Version, copyright © 1987, 1988 by Word Publishing, Dallas, Texas 75039. Used by permission.

Library of Congress Cataloging-in-Publication Data
Cherry, Reginald B.
Healing prayer : God's divine intervention in medicine, faith, and prayer / Reginald Cherry.
p. cm.
ISBN 0-7852-6940-1 (hc)
ISBN 0-7852-6751-4 (pb)
1. Spiritual healing. 2. Medicine—Religious aspects—Christianity. 3. Prayer—Christianity—Psychology. I. Title.
BT732.5.C486 1999
234'.131—dc21   99-039351

This book is dedicated to my great God, who is not only my Creator but also my Father. It is dedicated to His precious Son, Jesus, the anointed One, who bore in His own body not only my sins but also my diseases and infirmities.

I also dedicate this book to my precious friend, partner, and wife, Linda, whose prayers drew me to God and made me a joint heir with His Son.

CONTENTS

ACKNOWLEDGMENTS

The research for this book involved the endeavors of many Christian friends. I am deeply grateful for the research, writing, and editing of Jim Kerby, who assisted me in conveying the message that I believe will be life-changing for you and all of those who incorporate the words of this book into their lives. Thank you, Jim, for your skill, persistence, and prayers.

I also wish to acknowledge the encouragement and teaching of my beloved pastor, John H. Osteen, who is now with Jesus. His introducing me to the Word of God changed my life forever.

I wish to thank Thomas Nelson Publishers for their confidence in me and their desire to help people the world over attain a deeper understanding of the healing power of our precious Father in heaven.

Finally, I wish to acknowledge the prayers and support of our many viewers and partners who have supported us through our television ministry all of these years. May this book be a tool to help you and your family and to touch those who are suffering in their physical bodies or may have a spiritual need to know God personally.

INTRODUCTION

There are lots of sick people in the world today.

As we enter a new millennium, there are still multiplied millions living in Third World "developing" nations who are ravaged by the deadly effects of starvation, malnutrition, lack of clean water, poor sanitation, and uncontrolled vermin and insects. Progress is being made, although too slowly. Thank God for all who are working to stamp out such epidemics of wholesale misery.

But the sick people I'm talking about don't live in Third World countries. They live right here in America and in other modern, affluent nations with full access to the newest and best medical care available anywhere.

Yet, despite the amazing growth of medical technology and the development of new and more effective pharmaceuticals—despite state-of-the-art hospitals, clinics, and medical specialists paid for by publicly and privately funded health care insurance—there seem to be more people suffering from sickness and disease than ever before. How does one explain our society's failure to be cured and get healthier?

Not only are sick people turning to conventional medical care in their quest for pain control and cures for various maladies, they're reaching out to alternative and "fringe area" treatments as well. Psychic readings, transcendental meditation, crystals, aromatherapy, iridology, and related "therapies" are in widespread use. At the same time, an avalanche of patent medicines—pills of all kinds, potions, lotions, drops, and creams—are sold daily. Health stores display a bewildering array of organic foods, vitamins, minerals, herbs, supplements, and natural substances, as well as magnets, metal jewelry, and various paraphernalia with supposed curative qualities. What really works? What's just a fad?

Bookstores and newsstands sell thousands of different magazines, books, tapes, and videos on diet schemes, nutrition plans, wellness programs, and exercise regimes. Sales of health club memberships and home-use exercise equipment continue to flourish.

The fact that these kinds of enterprises are such big business and attract so many eager customers testifies to the number of unhealthy, unhappy, dissatisfied people who are searching for something—anything—to make them feel better. What is keeping them sick? Why can't they get well?

I believe there are more sick and diseased people in this country desperate to find help and hope than ever before. I'd venture to say that you wouldn't have to get out of your own family or neighborhood to find at least one person who is frustrated and frightened by a personal health crisis—with no answer in sight.

FRUSTRATED DOCTORS

Patients aren't the only ones who are frustrated. Doctors are often baffled and anxious when they run into one dead end after another in seeking the proper treatment for patients. Most physicians don't just go through the motions—they genuinely want to stop suffering and help restore health to the people they treat.

But what is a physician to do when a patient's case history and test results are inconclusive? Or which of the 150 different medications available for a particular condition should the physician choose?

What's the answer for a doctor when he's done everything he knows to do, tried every reasonable treatment, and prescribed the best medications available, but the patient isn't getting any better? How do you explain to parents expecting you to stop their child's pain that you don't know why the child is still hurting and nothing you've tried has worked? What is a patient to do after going to six doctors and getting six different opinions?

As a medical doctor, I am keenly aware that I am only a helper in the healing process. After I've diagnosed the likely cause of an illness, prescribed the appropriate medication or treatment, and explained the process to the patient, there's precious little else I personally can do. The real, actual healing is beyond my control. More than anyone else involved, I realize and acknowledge that the patient's recovery is up to a higher power.

So what is left for me to do? I pray! In fact, I pray during every part of the process—for inspiration, for wisdom, for revelation, for guidance, for healing.

I am part of a growing number of physicians who pray for and with their patients. With few exceptions, my patients want and appreciate prayer. It calms and assures them. It gives hope and bolsters their faith to expect and participate in the healing process.

Does prayer provide just a mental and emotional boost? Is its effect psychosomatic, a kind of placebo? Or is it for real—actually efficacious?

Is there real proof that prayer works, something besides anecdotes, hope-so, maybe-so, oral tradition? Has any respected researcher conducted scientific, controlled, foolproof tests?

As a matter of fact, yes. There have been scores of carefully designed and conducted studies on the effects of prayer in different medical settings over the last several decades, especially in the last thirty years. And the overwhelming, undeniable results of the majority of the tests prove that prayer works. Time and again prayer produced positive, significant, measurable results.

If prayer is therapeutically effective, why has it not been more widely practiced by medical practitioners? Why have the results of hundreds of scientific studies been hidden from public view for so long? Why is prayer making a "comeback" in just the last few years, with growing emphasis now?

These are just a few of the issues I attempt to address in this book. I also share some of my personal experiences and provide information that I hope will help you to find answers to other questions you may have as we go along.

For example, should you practice healing prayer for yourself and others? Does your physician pray with you? If not, would you like your physician to pray with you? How does one learn to pray for healing? Do you have to qualify or meet certain conditions in order to pray effectively?

Also, are there specific techniques for healing prayer? Do you just say, "Please heal me," or are there specific, detailed, directed petitions and intercessions? What are the best times, places, and ways to pray? What about praying for children or older people? For those with terminal diseases?

Do you have other questions about praying for healing? Good. I invite you to join me in a careful, honest look at the evidence, both scientific and spiritual. We'll look at the literature and the history. We'll examine some medical case histories. I'll help you conduct your own personal prayer development. See for yourself what others are discovering about prayer. Put prayer to the test.

At the end, you'll have a great deal of information to use in making up your own mind.

One man who honestly, openly explored this subject ended up praying this moving prayer:

My Lord and my God, I have a thousand arguments against Healing Prayer. You are the one argument for it . . . You win. Help me to be a conduit through which your healing love can flow to others. For Jesus' sake. Amen.[1]

1

THE SUPERNATURAL CONNECTION

From the beginning of human history, human beings have known that they were not alone in the universe. Archaeological studies of very early sites indicate that pre-historic man was aware of the supernatural—something or somebody bigger than himself or his finite powers, a force that transcended both the boundaries of his understanding and the physical limits of the world as he knew it. Deep within humanity was a consistent theme: the whole was somehow greater than the sum of the parts.

While I certainly don't regard myself as a qualified expert in anthropology or the history of world religions, I am very interested in man's supernatural connection. Like a great many other people, I've been curious about what the world was like for our ancient forebears and how their spiritual lifestyle developed. I've found that there is a great deal of information available to even the casual student through books, magazines, and excellent educational television programs and video series.

Among the most ancient artifacts of primitive cultures are obvious attempts to represent or depict a particular god or some form of deity. Every society seemed to worship something beyond themselves. Idols, totems, altars, and sacred dwellings of the gods—whether markers before "holy" mountains, trees, and rivers, or man-made temples—were part of almost every society's defining identity.

Animists saw virtually all living creatures, as well as rocks and trees, as gods. Some religions, like Hinduism, over the centuries recognized and embraced multiplied thousands of deities. Other cultures came to believe in a more centralized supernatural power, often acknowledged as the creator or source of all things, who was either a singular force or a select group of major deities.

Discovering that he had only limited control of the events and circumstances of his life, man instinctively assumed that a higher power controlled what happened to him. So from early on, man attempted to influence that power to obtain more favorable treatment through rituals designed to gain the attention and approval of deity, and often through offerings or sacrifices intended to please or appease "the gods." People sought divine assistance to escape the destructive effects of wind, rain, lightning, cold, heat, floods, or drought. They sought favor for hunting game, growing crops, and using natural resources.

And quite naturally, man pleaded for divine favor in obtaining healing and health for himself and his loved ones.

MAN'S URGE TO PRAY

In this seeking and pleading, the human family invented—or perhaps more accurately, discovered—prayer, a basic form of communication between man and a supernatural, "absolute" power. "The urge to pray seems so constant and widespread throughout history, it appears to be innate," said

Dr. Larry Dossey in his important book *Healing Words: The Power of Prayer and the Practice of Medicine.*[1]

Carol Osman Brown, writing in *HealthLinks* magazine, said, "The origins of prayer are lost in antiquity, but there is no known culture that does not use prayer in some form. In numerous world cultures healers, whether physicians, medicine men or psychic healers, all use some form of prayerful intervention in their work."[2]

An eminent English scientist, Sir Francis Galton, conducted one of the first objective inquiries into the efficacy of prayer and published his findings in the *Fortnightly Review* in 1872. Undertaking his study "for the satisfaction of [his] own conscience," Galton declared that the most persuasive reason to believe that prayer works is the indisputable fact that everyone uses it, pagans and orthodox believers alike. If prayer is not efficacious, he asked, why would it be universal?[3] A good question. If prayer didn't work, why wasn't it abandoned long ago?

Over the centuries, a virtually unlimited number of religions in every part of the world developed myriad ceremonies, rituals, and practices that invoked the positive involvement of deity in people's daily lives. For a great host of people, including the overwhelming majority of Americans, this meant developing a relationship with the God of Abraham, Isaac, and Jacob. Any study of Judeo-Christian literature and history reveals a wealth of emphatic teachings about and historic accounts of God's frequent supernatural intervention in the affairs of His people, the Hebrews, and those who later followed the teachings of Jesus Christ.

While Judaism, Christianity, Islam, and possibly a few other religions believed in a single deity, many others embraced multiple gods. For example, the New Testament account of

Paul the Apostle's appearance before the Areopagus in Athens reports that he was troubled at seeing that the city was full of idols.

Speaking on Mars Hill before this council of important Greek leaders, he challenged them for being "too superstitious." "I was going through your city, and I saw the things you worship. I found an altar that had these words written on it: 'TO A GOD WHO IS NOT KNOWN'" (Acts 17:23 NCV). Apparently the Athenians tried to worship every god they knew about and, taking no chances, even had an altar for any unknown deity they might have overlooked.

Many observers feel we presently live in a more secular society, with fewer people actively practicing the principles and teachings of any faith. Charles Colson, in his book *The Body: Being Light in Darkness*, suggests that America (and other Western nations) are now part of a "post Christian culture."[4] This may well be true. However, there is no apparent lessening of modern man's interest and hunger for involvement in the supernatural.

- There is a heightened fascination with the occult, with sales of books, magazines, and ritual paraphernalia skyrocketing, and related clubs and groups attracting millions of people from all walks of life.
- The "New Age" has become a vast, international industry, producing every kind of music, literature, schools, clothing, and religious practices imaginable.
- Crystals are touted as having near-miraculous spiritual properties to effect mental and physical healing when they are carried, worn, or put under the user's pillow at night. Witches, psychics, and channelers utilize them in various pagan ceremonies and practices.

- Using television to advertise and promote paid appointments for psychic readings is a multimillion-dollar enterprise.
- Movies and television programs with story lines about supernatural forces and practices attract ever-increasing audiences.

SPIRITUAL MATTERS AND THE MEDICAL WORLD

Early practitioners of the healing arts were keenly aware of the connection between the human mind or spirit and the welfare of the physical body. The *Hippocratic Writings*, which date back two thousand years, observe that "there is a measure of conscious thought throughout the body."[5]

The legendary Persian physician Avicenna (A.D. 980–1037) declared, "The imagination of a man can act not only on his own body but even others and very distant bodies. It can fascinate and modify them; make them ill, or restore them to health."[6] Plato said, "The great error in the treatment of the human body is that physicians are ignorant of the whole. For the part can never be well unless the whole is well."[7]

Through the centuries, the history of medicine was the history of religion. Quaker theologian Richard Foster pointed out that the ancient Hebrews saw persons as a unity, and they found it unthinkable to minister to the body without ministering to the spirit, and vice versa. "The Pentateuch [the first five books of the Old Testament] contained detailed stipulations about going to the priest whenever disease was suspected (Lev. 13ff.)," Foster noted. "Even in many 'primitive' cultures today the doctor and the priest are one and the same person."[8]

So when and how did modern medicine come to separate and de-emphasize the spiritual aspect of man in its care and treatment of patients?

In the 1600s, the French philosopher Descartes separated mind from body, influencing medical science to begin describing disease in terms of environmental agents, germs, or wayward genes, independently of the mind. Dale A. Matthews, M.D., associate professor of medicine at Georgetown University School of Medicine, says that with "the discovery of pathogens [microorganisms such as bacilli, germs, viruses, and bacteria] . . . suddenly, medicine was biomedicine."[9] Disease and the healing of disease became based solely on natural things. This increased emphasis on physical science played down the importance of anything that could not be observed or measured.

Then, in the 1700s, Sir Isaac Newton described classical laws of matter and energy that dictated that the entire universe, including the human body, is a vast clockwork that functions according to deterministic, causal principles. This required that all forms of therapy, to be effective, must embody purely physical means. As a result, doctors increasingly began to view the body "scientifically" and mechanically. Essentially, for the next two hundred years, Western civilization tended to regard disease "as being more or less a function of the physical body and to look at thoughts, feelings, emotions and social interactions as being only the mind."[10] And according to Dossey, the effects of mind and consciousness were considered of secondary importance.[11]

This kind of attitude, which became the prevailing position of most medical practitioners in America, often produced clinicians who treated a patient like a throat, for example, rather than a person behind a throat. The whole emphasis was on finding a problem and "fixing" it with medicine, surgery, or other medical therapy rather than treating a whole person and helping him find healing. Medicine largely ignored spirituality and religion in patient management, at least officially.

The majority of doctors were so focused on the physical aspects of sickness and disease that they failed to consider the mental or spiritual part of the people they treated. Many physicians went so far as to suspect that patients who openly believed in spiritual things—who saw God as a personal Being who was interested in their health and welfare—were mentally deranged.

But if doctors downplayed the importance of the spiritual dimension, patients certainly did not. Numerous surveys and studies confirmed that a tremendous percentage of people who sought medical treatment continued to pray personally and to seek the prayers of others for their recovery. And a dramatic number of them wanted their doctors to acknowledge and accommodate the spiritual aspect of their care. These patients were often subjected to ridicule for even bringing up religious beliefs.

As early as 1988, medical researcher Harold Koenig noted: "High technology medicine is accomplishing much, but its limitations are obvious to many. It has emphasized the mechanical, physiological, and biochemical means for restoring health and sustaining physical life, but it has tended to minimize or even ignore the psychological, social, and especially the religious and spiritual dimensions of healing."[12]

For at least the last several decades, many doctors were aware of patients' faith in prayer and dependence on spirituality in their self-care. Belief and faith have been known for many years to have an impact on health and disease. Indeed, Sir William Osler, one of the fathers of modern medicine, wrote about "the faith that heals" more than seventy-five years ago. And other physicians privately acknowledged that they had witnessed the remarkable and unexplainable recovery of patients from conditions and diseases for which there was no effective medical therapy. These were generally noted as curious anomalies.

However, some well-known medical authorities were quite outspoken. Hints of the power in the spirit world began to emerge from secular sources. The famous Swiss psychologist, Carl Jung, declared: "During the past 30 years, people from all the civilized countries of the earth have consulted me. I have treated many hundreds of patients . . . Among all my patients in the second half of life—that is to say, over 35—there has not been one whose problem in the last resort was not that of finding a religious outlook on life. It is safe to say that every one of them fell ill because he had lost that which the living religions of every age have given to their followers, and none of them has really been healed who did not regain his religious outlook."[13]

Perhaps no one realized the full extent of the population's religious convictions and its belief in the power of prayer for healing and health. In 1996, *Time* magazine did a cover story on the subject and reported the results of a major poll it had conducted. The poll found that 82 percent of adult Americans believed in the healing power of personal prayer, 73 percent believed praying for someone can help cure their illness, and 64 percent believed doctors should pray with patients if requested to.[14]

The next year *Newsweek* confirmed the findings with its

own poll, in which 79 percent of respondents who said they prayed regularly declared that they believed God answers prayers for healing.[15]

Obviously, by the last decade of the century, there was strong evidence that the "medicine is strictly science" tide had turned. An article in the *American Medical News* noted a "widening dissatisfaction among physicians with what they view as an increasingly depersonalized practice."[16] *The Lancet*, a British medical publication, reported: "Of 296 physicians surveyed during the October, 1996, meeting of the American Academy of Family Physicians, 99% were convinced that religious beliefs can heal, and 75% believed that prayers of others could promote a patient's recovery."[17]

Trying to be sensitive to the needs of their patients, more and more doctors began moving to again combine the healing streams of medicine and prayer. Many were being motivated by the continuing emergence of a tremendous body of evidence in the form of qualified scientific studies that support such action.

Dr. Larry Dossey says he stumbled onto the information in the 1980s—"controlled studies showing that prayer has positive effects even when tested under stringent conditions in double-blind studies in hospitals and laboratories. These studies involved not only humans but non-humans as well. I was tremendously impressed by this and spent years chasing down every study I could find. One hundred thirty one studies later, I concluded this is one of the best kept secrets in modern medicine."[18]

Epidemiologist Jeff Levin, a research fellow at the National Institute for Healthcare Research, reviewed more than two hundred medical studies dating back to the nineteenth century. He concluded that religious commitment enhances

11

health and that evidence shows prayer plays a therapeutic role in disease. "In fact," he added, "a lack of spirituality seems to be a risk factor for higher rates of illness."[19]

Georgetown University's Dr. Dale Matthews also reported that in the overwhelming majority of studies he has researched "there is a positive relationship between religious and spiritual commitment and health, especially in the areas of substance abuse, mental illness, quality of life, and survival."[20]

How could such convincing proof have been ignored for so long? As Dossey noted in his book *Healing Words*, "A body of knowledge that does not fit with prevailing ideas can be ignored as if it does not exist, no matter how scientifically valid it may be. Scientists, including physicians, can have blind spots in their vision. The power of prayer, it seemed, was an example."[21]

PUTTING PRAYER UNDER A MICROSCOPE

In recent years, however, researchers have been making up for lost time, not only revisiting early studies but conducting a great many new ones. "Foundations, government agencies, teaching hospitals, and universities are now sponsoring numerous studies testing scientific evidence for the efficacy of prayer," said Gary Thomas in a 1997 article in *Christianity Today*. "Academics are developing and administering well-designed and -respected studies aimed at establishing a scientifically discernible link between prayer and healing."[22]

A Christian cardiologist, Dr. Randolph Byrd, conducted

the landmark study in 1984 that led to the resurgence of scientific evaluation of the effect of prayer on healing. Over a ten-month period, 393 patients admitted to the coronary care unit at San Francisco General Hospital were computer-assigned to either a 201-patient control group or to the 192 patients who were prayed for daily by five to seven people in home prayer groups. The test was a randomized, double-blind experiment in which neither the patients, nurses, nor doctors knew which group the patients were in.

At the study's conclusion, Byrd discovered a definite pattern of obvious differences between the control group and those prayed for:

1. Those prayed for were five times less likely to require antibiotics.
2. They were three times less likely to develop pulmonary edema, a condition in which the lungs fill with fluid.
3. None of those prayed for required endotracheal intubation, the insertion of an artificial airway in the throat, compared with twelve in the control group who required the treatment.
4. They experienced fewer cases of pneumonia and cardiopulmonary arrests.
5. Fewer patients in the prayed-for group died.[23]

Today Byrd's study is regarded as extremely significant. Dr. Dossey frequently refers to it and says, "If the technique being studied had been a new drug or a surgical procedure instead of prayer, it would almost certainly have been heralded as some sort of 'breakthrough.'"[24]

Dossey also commented that even hard-boiled skeptics recognize the importance of Byrd's work. Dr. William Nolan, who wrote a book debunking faith healing, is quoted as saying, "It sounds like this study will stand up to scrutiny . . . maybe we doctors ought to be writing on our order sheets, 'Pray three times a day.' If it works, it works."[25]

I had a special personal interest in the news of this study when it was published in 1988. I attended premed with Randolph Byrd, shared classes with him, and knew him well. His medical knowledge, professional integrity, and quiet Christian testimony were exemplary.

SUBSEQUENT STUDIES

Since Byrd's study, the number of related scientific experiments has continued to grow. The results of numerous new studies on the benefits of religion and spirituality are being released regularly. In a December 1998 article in the *Journal of the American Medical Association (JAMA)*, Mike Mitka commented on the number of recent research articles available to physicians wanting to incorporate spirituality into their treatment arsenal.

JAMA referred specifically to:

- A Duke University project that found people who attended religious services at least once a week and prayed or studied the Bible at least daily had consistently lower blood pressure than those who did so less frequently or not at all.
- A study headed by Duke's Harold Koenig, M.D., that found that among elderly patients suffering from depression related to hospitalization for a physical illness, the more spiritual they were, the quicker they reached remission from depression.

- A study of 1,718 older adults in North Carolina that indicated elderly people who regularly attend church have healthier immune systems than those who don't.
- A fourth study that found that patients aged sixty or older who attended church weekly or more often were significantly less likely to have been admitted to the hospital, had fewer acute-hospital admissions, and spent fewer days in the hospital during the previous year than those who attended church less often.[26]

The *Journal of the National Cancer Institute* reported that studies indicate many cancer patients, in particular, rely on religion and spirituality after their diagnosis. In a University of Michigan study, 93 of 106 women under treatment for various stages of uterine and ovarian cancer said their religious lives helped them sustain hope. Edward Creagan, M.D., of the Division of Medical Oncology at the Mayo Clinic in Rochester, Minnesota, said that "among the coping methods of long-term cancer survivors, the predominant strategy is spiritual."[27]

Yet another spiritual-body relationship was suggested in a survey of 400 patients in Georgia in 1989, according to *Forbes* magazine. Those who believed religion was very important had lower diastolic blood pressure readings than those who did not.[28]

A 1997 *American Journal of Public Health* article about a twenty-eight-year study of more than 5,000 California subjects reported convincing findings that frequent churchgoers were more likely to live longer than people who went to church less frequently.[29]

MEDICINE'S NEW APPROACH

In 1999 a study reported in the *Journal of Gerontology* found that individuals who regularly attended church services lived 28 percent longer than those in the study who did not regularly attend church. This percentage of longevity is the same as that of nonsmokers compared to smokers!

When I was attending the University of Texas Medical School in the early 1970s, there were no courses on spirituality and religion. I believe this was universally the case at all the nation's 126 medical schools. Now, at least a third of U.S. medical schools have integrated "spirituality education" into the required portion of their curricula, and more than 50 now offer elective courses.[30] By the turn of the century, some authorities expect that nearly all medical schools will have done so.[31]

Dr. Dale Matthews is at the forefront of modern scientific research into the healing power of prayer. As I mentioned, not only has he conducted his own experiments and reported their results, he has surveyed 325 other studies on spirituality and health. His verdict? "Religion is good medicine," he declared. "Seventy-five percent of [the studies] show faith is beneficial."[32]

According to *Christianity Today*, "The recent interest in prayer and healing has spawned a new descriptor. Dr. Larry Burk of Duke University uses the phrase 'complementary medicine.' Complementary medicine seeks to combine prayer and traditional medical practice rather than pit the two against each other. This is in contrast to 'alternative medicine' (anything from yoga and EST to aromatherapy), which has largely been devoid of Christian faith . . . and often pits itself against traditional medicine."[33]

16

Dr. Myles Sheehan, a Jesuit priest who is assistant professor of medicine and geriatrics at Loyola University Medical Center, recently said, "Spiritual practices clearly are a complement to traditional medicine, and we should make every effort to incorporate our patients' spirituality to promote healing."[34]

Theologian Richard Foster agrees, noting that "always before, the physician of the body, the physician of the mind, and the physician of the spirit were the same person . . . So it is with enthusiasm that we applaud the demise of the heretical tendency to fragment and compartmentalize human beings."[35]

Herbert Benson, M.D., is a behavioral medicine specialist at the prestigious Harvard University in Cambridge, Massachusetts. After twenty years of work in this field, he is considered a visionary leader in a new approach to medicine—one where the patient's faith, or belief system, is as important as pills.

"Science is showing us how mind and body, body and mind are inseparable," says Dr. Benson. He describes his mix of biology and belief as a three-legged stool. One leg is pharmaceutical. One is surgical. The third leg is self-care.

"When we bring that third leg in, we have truly balanced our approach," he says. Nutrition, exercise, and stress management are part of that balancing leg. So are spirituality and faith.[36]

The supernatural connection is real. It can be traced back to the days of history. Today it is being studied by the high-tech world of modern medicine. Using the techniques of medical science, man's greatest supernatural power—the power of prayer—is proving to be a vital factor in the healing of our bodies.

2

COMPLEMENTARY HEALING SOURCES: THE NATURAL SIDE

At present, more than 325 studies have been done on the role of "spirituality and health." According to Dr. Dale Matthews, 75 percent of the studies show faith is beneficial. These studies are radical in many aspects.

First of all, the fact that scientific dollars would be devoted to the study of prayer and faith as it affects healing is astounding. I am sure many of the researchers enter into these studies trying to disprove the role of spirituality and to demonstrate it to be a myth.

The second and even more astounding finding is the fact that over 75 percent of the studies show a positive and consistent healing association with prayer, faith, churchgoing, and the healing of disease. This has truly revolutionized medicine. In the last two or three continuing medical education conferences that I have attended, spirituality was addressed. In fact, whole conferences are now being devoted to the subject of what is called "complementary/alternative medicine." We will study in a later chapter that just being spiritual, however, is very different from following the Bible guidelines that Jesus taught concerning prayer for the sick and healing.

We are also discovering something about prayer that many people have not considered: prayer has a supernatural component as God's healing anointing and power overcome disease in the body, but it can also offer an individual a specific direction to take in the natural world that leads to healing. In our medical practice, we have discovered that healing sometimes is manifested supernaturally and instantaneously (who in the world wouldn't want it this way?). But healing often is a combination of the supernatural power of knowing how to pray specifically for disease combined with God's healing anointing as it flows through natural substances.

God prepared us for this centuries ago, when He said in Exodus 23 that before disease would be taken from our midst, His blessing would first be on our bread and water (that is, what we eat). Another important Scripture is Proverbs 18:9: "He who does not use his endeavors to heal himself is brother to him who commits suicide" (AMPLIFIED). In other words, there is often a practical side of healing that we must pursue with all diligence, just as we enter into the supernatural side of healing by presenting our prayers and petitions before God according to Philippians 4:6.

The incredible healing recorded in John 9, where Jesus touched a blind man with mud and saliva, brings up several interesting questions. One would think that any time Jesus touched someone, the person would be healed instantly and supernaturally. In this case, that was not true. The blind man wasn't healed instantly after Jesus touched him. Instead, Jesus gave the man a set of specific instructions to follow. The man did not question Jesus, argue with Him, or challenge Him for instant supernatural healing (such as Bartimaeus received in Mark 10). The blind man simply obeyed and followed a path down to a pool of water. Then as Jesus had instructed him, he reached down in the pool, washed the mud and saliva from his eyes and, as John 9:7 (KJV) says, as he went *his way*, he was healed. He was just as healed as Bartimaeus, who was touched supernaturally by Jesus and instantly healed, but his *pathway to healing* was different.

I am thankful for the supernatural, instantaneous healings that occurred under Jesus' ministry and that still happen today. God's instruction to me, however, has been to have people consider carefully whether their healing may involve the combination of the supernatural as well as the natural. I believe healing comes from God, and thus is supernatural. Of all the healings recorded in the Bible, isn't it interesting that the mud and saliva pathway to healing was included by the Holy Spirit? I believe this particular account opens the door for us to pray a specific prayer of healing, seeking our unique pathway to healing. We must be willing to accept that our pathway to healing can be supernatural and instantaneous, but it may also, and often does, involve the supernatural combined with the natural.

Of all the laws given under the old covenant (Old Testament), one in every three dealt with health instructions to the Israelites. Frequently these concerned nutrition practices. In my years of medical practice as a Christian physician, I have become convinced that many Christians fail to receive their healing because they do not realize that healing can involve the supernatural as well as the natural. I believe that when we do what we can do under the leading of the Holy Spirit, then God does what we cannot do.

As we discussed in Chapter 1, compelling research from secular sources consistently supports the power of prayer in healing. In this chapter we will consider secular sources that parallel the biblical teaching that healing anointing can flow through natural chemicals created by God.

As James S. Gordon explained, "No matter what you call it, a medical revolution is radically changing American health care . . . [Experts estimate that] more than 40 percent of all Americans use some form of alternative or non-traditional healing techniques. Increasingly, doctors and health care practitioners are integrating the precision of modern science with ancient healing techniques."[1]

The sale of vitamins, food supplements, herbs, and other plant-derived "natural" substances and compounds has become a multibillion-dollar business. We are seeing health food stores the size of supermarkets becoming commonplace. Thousands of marketing firms are now appearing on the Internet, offering every kind of alternative healing product imaginable. The U.S. market is seeing more than $10 billion a year in sales of herbs and other natural substances. Amazingly, this expenditure is increasing at the rate of 15 percent per year.

In Europe, the use of natural substances is even greater than in the United States, with several billion dollars in sales annually. These substances often are dispensed by the prescription of medical practitioners. Phytochemicals (plant-derived chemicals) are mainstream medicinals in Europe and actually are reimbursed as a part of standard medical care in Germany.

The "natural" substance and herbal supplement industry has grown so rapidly that much confusion has resulted, with extravagant and often untruthful claims being made about many products. Unfortunately, mainstream medical doctors and other health practitioners have been slow to react to the growing availability of alternative or nontraditional healing techniques and to inform themselves of the true benefits (as well as the harmful effects) of natural substances.

A common objection by physicians to the use of phyto-chemicals, herbal substances, and vitamins is that they "have not been studied enough." Many physicians are not aware of the World Health Organization (WHO) policy statement that was issued in 1993, which reads, "The historic use of an herbal is a valid form of information on safety and efficacy in the absence of scientific evidence to the contrary." In other words, if an herbal-type ingredient has been used for decades or even centuries by multiple and diverse groups of people, this does, in fact, represent a valid form of evidence to its safety. It also is an indication that the ingredients in the herb (whatever they might be) are indeed helpful and useful even though stringent scientific studies are not available.

Many herbal substances, unlike prescription drugs, are not subject to patent. A so-called valid scientific study (known by doctors as a longitudinal, double-blind, placebo-controlled, crossover study) is not possible because these studies can cost in excess of $20 million. On the other hand, saw palmetto, for example, has been used by Native American Indian tribes for centuries for prostate problems. In recent years we have discovered that there is indeed a chemical in the saw palmetto plant exactly like that in one of our modern prescription medicines that can shrink prostate tissue and increase urinary flow. The fact that saw palmetto has been used by multiple groups of people for the same purpose without ill effects and that people who use it today notice the same beneficial effect is sufficient evidence that we can incorporate it into our modern medical practices. Still, doctors are very slow to accept this basic concept.

Even though physicians are often quick to put down medicines that are derived from plants (although nearly 50 percent of our prescription medicines are), they cannot argue that some of the most commonly used medications in medicine were originally plant-derived. The foxglove plant, for example, yielded digitalis, which has been a medical mainstay in the treatment of congestive heart failure and heart rhythm disturbances. Other common medicines used today that were derived from plants include psyllium, senna, atropine, morphine, scopolamine, and numerous others.

For much of this century, merchants of "natural" health products and practitioners of alternative therapies have been shunned by the medical community. Many physicians have regarded them with extreme suspicion, viewing them as little more than snake oil salesmen or scam artists. In truth, there often has been good reason for skepticism of some of the fads, the excessive claims, and the emphasis on New Age mysticism associated with health food stores. As a physician with a busy medical practice, I frequently hear horror stories from my patients about some of the suggestions they have received about natural treatments.

Yet no one can deny the genuine healing qualities of many natural substances. The folk medicine of America's mountain and rural populations and the tribal lore of Native Indian healers and medicine men often included flowers, plants, trees, leaves, roots, and fruits that proved curative for their various diseases. Though much mysticism surrounded the use of many of these natural plants, there is no denying that they were beneficial. The use of herbs, foods, and minerals for medicinal purposes dates back thousands of years. Today's medical studies are continuing to reveal more and more the benefit of these plants and the substances derived from them.

God has provided healing for us! In fact, if we rightly divide the Word of God, we discover that we *were* healed two thousand years ago as Jesus bore our sins, iniquities, and infirmities on the cross through His own blood (see 1 Peter 2:24; Matt. 8:17; Isa. 53:5). If healing is indeed an accomplished thing, many ask then, "Why am I still sick in my body?" The reason is that we are not praying specifically for the *manifestation* of healing that Jesus has already purchased in His body. To realize this manifestation of healing, we must combine the "effective, fervent prayer of a righteous man" according to James 5:16 (NKJV) with the information God is revealing to us about healing anointing as it flows through natural substances that He created for the benefit of man.

In a later chapter, we will share actual case histories from our Christian medical practice that demonstrate how the use of prayer, natural substances, or a combination of the two helped patients receive the manifestation of healing in their bodies. Here, let me list some common diseases that you or your family may face and God's natural provision for overcoming them. Remember, very often the use of natural substances must be combined with the power of specific prayer for that disease to see healing manifested.

ALZHEIMER'S DISEASE

An exciting scientific study on a traditional herbal remedy was recently presented in October 1997 in one of the most prestigious medical journals. The substance is called *Egb 761*, and it is extracted from the ancient Chinese tree ginkgo biloba. To my knowledge, it was one of the first so-called natural substances to be highlighted in the highly regarded *Journal of the American Medical Association (JAMA)*. The substance derived from ginkgo has been used by the Chinese for centuries for treating impaired circulation, memory loss, dementia, and ringing in the ears; it also is reported to produce certain learning-enhancing effects. It has been used in Europe for "cerebral insufficiency," which is a form of memory loss. More than $200 million worth of ginkgo extract is sold in Europe each year. The *JAMA* article reported on a study of 309 patients in multiple medical centers who were administered the extract from ginkgo biloba (Egb 761). According to the report, Egb 761 appeared to stabilize and improve the dementia and memory loss in people with moderate to severe Alzheimer's disease.

The scientists, led by Dr. Pierre L. LeBars of the New York Institute for Medical Research, reported that "compared with the placebo group, the Egb group included twice as many patients whose cognitive performance improved and half as many whose social function worsened." In simple terms, twice as many people experienced improved memory function on the ginkgo and half as many experienced a decline in their social interaction with others.[2]

The total daily dosage of ginkgo biloba was between 160 and 240 mg, divided into at least two doses. It took six weeks before effects began to occur.

While certainly this is not a cure for Alzheimer's disease, the use of this extract is an encouraging development. The Egb study, added to European studies showing that ginkgo helps treat Alzheimer's disease (which is, incidentally, the most common form of dementia), will most likely spur greater use of ginkgo as a treatment for the disease in the United States.[3] Ginkgo definitely increases blood flow to the brain, and I have added this to my personal daily supplement intake as a preventive measure.

Isn't it amazing that a well-accepted medical journal featured a report on an ancient, natural alternative medical substance! This is a sign that medical doctors are becoming more open and receptive to any remedy or treatment that will help and not harm their patients.

Other natural substances that benefit Alzheimer's disease include *vitamin E* and natural plant-derived *estrogens*. We do not know the exact cause of Alzheimer's, but it is suspected that it is related to what are known as "free radicals" caused by the metabolism and breakdown of oxygen in the body. Antioxidants such as *vitamin E, vitamin C, selenium,* and *beta-carotene* can help protect the body from various degenerative diseases, and we recommend them as part of a comprehensive supplement program as a precaution.

Several studies have demonstrated that estrogen will also retard, delay, or even prevent Alzheimer's disease. Many of the commonly prescribed estrogens, however, have numerous potential problems, and we are currently recommending a natural plant-derived estrogen containing substances known as isoflavones. Soy is an example of a plant that contains two prominent natural estrogens, but a plant known as red clover contains all four of the primary natural isoflavones. Again, studies have not been done on these substances with regard to Alzheimer's disease, but there is strong suggestive evidence that their similarity to prescription estrogen will also provide a protection from Alzheimer's disease.

A big advantage of using these substances is that they help protect a woman from breast cancer, uterine cancer, and osteoporosis, as well as heart disease, while alleviating many postmenopausal symptoms, such as hot flashes, that women may experience as they go through menopause.

CANCER

We do not fully understand cancer, but we do know that it is basically a failure of the body's immune system. Interestingly, many researchers believe that cancer occurs weekly in all of us, but a strong immune system quickly recognizes and suppresses abnormal cells. Though cancer is probably the most feared disease, it ranks well behind heart and vascular disease in occurrence.[4]

The traditional approach of physicians has been to wait until cancer occurs and then cut it out (surgery), burn it out (radiation), or poison it (chemotherapy). Even though some of these techniques can be effective for certain types of cancer, they essentially cause multiple side effects even though they can (temporarily) shrink cancers. The problem is that they can never remove every last cancer cell from the body, and when administered they cause damage to normal cells. In fact, these treatments can weaken the immune system that God designed to fight cancer.

The good news is we are seeing increasing research in medical journals demonstrating that certain diets can prevent and attack cancer. There are also various herbs, vitamins, minerals, and other natural products that not only can prevent but also can destroy abnormal cancer cells. This is God's "chemotherapy." I want to give you a sampling of some of the natural substances that are showing a consistent, positive effect on cancer.

Prostate Cancer Breakthroughs

Selenium, a trace element often found in certain grains and certain types of meat and fish, has been tested in multiple scientific studies. One interesting study set out to determine whether selenium would have a positive effect on skin cancer. Results showed conclusively that of the 1,312 patients studied, the supplement didn't do much for skin cancer. But halfway through the study, researchers began noticing an amazing affect. Those in the selenium-supplemented group had a 37 percent reduction in other types of cancer incidence and a 50 percent reduction in cancer death or mortality compared to the control group that was not getting selenium. One of the most astounding findings was that the test group had 63 percent fewer prostate cancers, 58 percent fewer colorectal cancers, and 46 percent fewer lung cancers.[5]

According to Dr. Larry C. Clark, who headed the experiment at the Arizona Cancer Center in Tucson, Arizona, "The results of this study are exciting because they show the cancer preventive potential of a nutritional supplement [added] to a normal diet."[6] The appropriate dose for selenium as used in prostate cancer prevention is 200 mcg daily.

Vitamin E, simple and commonly available, has also been shown to prevent prostate cancer and seems to work even better when combined with selenium. Prostate cancer is a major killer of men in developed, industrialized countries. Studies have shown that well over half of all men who reach age eighty have microscopic cancer cells in their prostate (though they may not necessarily die of prostate cancer). Of course, we men don't want any prostate cancer cells in our prostate gland, and that's why I'm sharing this information with you!

A test in Finland of 29,133 men who took daily doses of vitamin E for five to eight years showed they had 32 percent less symptomatic prostate cancer, according to a report in the *Journal of the National Cancer Institute.*[7] Researchers have found that vitamin E, because it is an antioxidant, may attack free radical formation and inhibit the transformation of latent, benign cancer cells into actual symptomatic disease. Vitamin E may also boost a person's immune system.[8]

Because prostate cancer is the most common cancer in a nonsmoking male, it is my recommendation that every man consider supplementing his diet with extra amounts of vitamin E and selenium. I recommend using the natural form of vitamin E rather than the synthetic form (the label on the bottle will indicate "natural" or "d-alpha"). An appropriate dose would be 400 to 800 IU daily. Though many of us don't want to take extra pills, even if they are vitamins, decreasing prostate cancer risk by up to 60 percent may make you change your mind.

COMMON FOODS THAT OFFER PROTECTION AND EVEN HEALING FROM CANCER

Interestingly, one of the most potent cancer-fighting compounds usually sits within arm's reach when we eat at restaurants. This ingredient is in the ketchup bottle, right beside the salt, sugar, and all of those other substances we've been told we should avoid. Ketchup contains a unique pigment known as *lycopene*. This red substance in tomatoes appears to trigger a tumor-suppressor chemical known as connexin 43. A study reported at the ninetieth annual meeting of the American Association for Cancer Research showed that this chemical had a marked effect of reducing prostate cancer. Evidence now indicates that this substance may also be effective against lung, stomach, pancreatic, bowel, breast, and cervical cancer.

Medical researchers in America and Britain have looked at seventy-two different studies from around the world and found that fifty-seven of these studies reported associations between tomato intake (lycopene intake) and reduced cancer. Lycopene has gained such prominence that it is now marketed in capsule form, and in several studies where two 15 mg capsules of a lycopene extract were used, tumor mass size decreased. Also, various chemical markers for cancer, such as PSA (in the case of prostate cancer), decreased dramatically, often in as little as three weeks!

Lycopene is an antioxidant and carotenoid and is most abundant in tomatoes, but it is also found in lesser amounts in watermelons and grapefruit. Researchers discovered that men who consumed high amounts of cooked tomatoes have the lowest rates of prostate cancer—up to 45 percent less. Raw tomatoes provide much less protection. This is a point that we should note carefully. Though we often think that raw vegetables and fruits are better for our health, there are exceptions. Processing and cooking tomatoes release the beneficial lycopene and provide much greater cancer-fighting protection than the raw substance. Cooked tomatoes also help the body absorb the compound better.

Another good source of lycopene from tomatoes is marinara sauce, commonly available in Italian restaurants. Although ketchup is fairly high in sodium, persons with normal blood pressure probably will benefit from the cancer protective effects anyway. Other good sources include tomato juice and tomato puree.

Garlic continues to prove itself as an extraordinarily

healthful food. Studies indicate that it contains as many as thirty cancer-fighting chemicals containing compounds such as *vitamins A* and *C, potassium, phosphorus, sulfur, selenium,* and several different *amino acids.* Epidemiological studies have found that in areas of the world where people eat a lot of garlic and onions (which are a cousin of garlic and contain many of the same beneficial substances, though in lesser amounts) there is decreased incidence of many types of cancers. According to an article distributed by the Mayo Foundation for Medical Education and Research, "The Iowa Women's Health Study found that, of all foods evaluated, garlic showed the strongest association with decreased risk for colon cancer."[9]

While garlic is not a guaranteed cancer-preventing agent, we do recommend it to patients, and I, in fact, take it myself. Garlic also has been shown to lower blood pressure, and it raises the level of the good or protective HDL cholesterol. You may lose some friends if you eat the natural cloves of garlic, due to the strong sulfur compounds, which will come out in your breath and skin. I prefer to take a garlic capsule daily. One advantage of the capsule is that it maintains steady, constant blood levels of the active allicin compounds in garlic. (And its lack of odor helps me retain my friends.)

CHRONIC FATIGUE SYNDROME

Nicotinamide adenine dinucleotide (NADH) is an over-the-counter, food-derived nutritional supplement reported to produce marked improvement in symptoms of Chronic Fatigue Syndrome. Although the exact cause of this debilitating condition—which is marked by fatigue so extreme that the patient may not be able to perform normal activities—is still unknown, current research seems to indicate that an overreaction of the body's immune system may be involved. The result is an imbalance that develops in a key energy-producing compound in the cells known as ATP (adenosine triphosphate), which affects muscle contraction and energy production. NADH is manufactured in the United States and is available without a prescription. Patients taking 10 mg of this food-derived nutritional supplement have reported marked improvement in their symptoms.

DIABETES

Chromium picolinate and *vanadium* are two trace minerals that have been proved effective in the treatment of diabetes. Recently published reports of three different studies on vanadium in Canada and Japan noted that it mimics the metabolic actions of insulin and significantly improves impaired glucose tolerance (a preliminary or precursor form of diabetes). Chromium picolinate also works with insulin to regulate the body's use of sugar and may also help suppress cardiovascular disease. Its possible effect on metabolism also makes it a helpful supplement in weight loss programs, though the research in this area is less definitive than in diabetes. Chromium also has an indirect effect on the immune system by stimulating T-lymphocytes and interferon.[10] In our treatment of diabetic patients, we will often use chromium picolinate, 200 to 1,000 mcg per day, and vanadyl sulfate, 50 mg three times daily.

DEPRESSION

St. John's Wort has become a popular herbal remedy for mild to moderate depression. It was included in a recent study of herbs used to treat psychiatric symptoms conducted at the Clarke Institute of Psychiatry in Toronto, Canada. A November 1998 report in the *Archives of General Psychiatry* found that "there was good evidence for the efficacy of St. John's Wort for the treatment of depression."[11] An earlier report in the *British Medical Journal* declared St. John's Wort to be equal to conventional antidepressives with significantly fewer side effects. This herbal remedy is prescribed frequently in Germany for the treatment of depression and, in fact, is used much more frequently than the typical prescription medication. Follow the dosage instructions on the bottle.

TENSION, ANXIETY, AND INSOMNIA

Valerian and *kava kava* are herbal treatments for tension, anxiety, and insomnia. One important study showed valerian root extract significantly reduced the time it took to fall asleep, and it also improved sleep quality as well as reducing nighttime awakening in persons suffering from insomnia. Kava kava is actually a member of the pepper family and has been used for some thirty centuries for its medicinal benefits in treating anxiety and nervous disorders. There are several dozen studies, primarily originating in Germany, that have shown it to be a mood elevator as well as a mild sedative. The active ingredient in kava kava was compared head-to-head with the prescription tranquilizer Valium and proved to be just as effective but had almost no side effects.

PROSTATE ENLARGEMENT

Saw palmetto and *pygeum* are popular natural treatments for the symptoms of prostate enlargement, which include increased frequency of urination, difficulty starting urination, weakness in the urinary stream, and failure to completely empty the bladder. Numerous studies have shown saw palmetto to be effective in treating benign prostatic hyperplasia (BPH), the noncancerous enlargement of the prostate, which is very common in men over the age of fifty. Though not quite as well known, pygeum is derived from the bark of a tree and contains a chemical known as beta-sitosterol, a chemical that reduces inflammation, swelling, and edema (fluid accumulation in the lower extremities). Extracts from pygeum bark have been shown to be as effective as prescription medications and are sometimes used in combination with saw palmetto.

CONGESTIVE HEART FAILURE AND CANCER

Coenzyme Q-10 is an antioxidant found in multiple plants, bran cereals, and other products, but it is also made in small amounts in the human body. This was originally used and found to be beneficial for congestive heart failure, and we still recommend it for our patients suffering from this increasingly common problem. More recently, researchers have used Co Q-10 in the treatment of cancer. Co Q-10 seems to strengthen and improve the pumping ability of the heart muscle, reducing the accompanying symptoms of shortness of breath, fluid buildup in the lower extremities, and the inability to lie flat. When used in cancer patients, Co Q-10 has been shown to reverse fluid accumulation in the lungs and has caused remission of cancer that has metastasized to the liver. The benefit in cancer patients seems to occur by its enhancing effects on the body's natural immune system.

ARTHRITIS

Glucosamine sulfate and *chondroitin sulfate* are natural substances that are having dramatic results in treating arthritis, particularly the most common variety of arthritis, osteoarthritis. We have become very familiar with these substances, but the fact of the matter is they work. Glucosamine stimulates the repair of cartilage while reducing inflammation in the joints. Although positive effects may not be evident for two to three months, regular daily usage has been proved to be as effective as prescription medicine for osteoarthritis. Chondroitin sulfate helps make the cartilage that lines joints more elastic by increasing water retention. It can also block enzymes that tend to destroy cartilage. Both substances are natural, effective, safe, and available without prescription. Simply follow the dosage on the bottle, which is generally a standardized dosage.

There are literally scores of other medically beneficial herbs, vitamins, and supplements available to us today. The scope of this book does not permit a comprehensive description of all of them and, in fact, many of them are just passing fads. Some are controversial and a few are actually dangerous.

We have taught about numerous other natural substances such as primrose oil, MSM, CMO, DLPA, and you will hear about more and more studies substantiating the usefulness of natural substances God produced for man. The physician of the future is going to be the doctor who has a knowledge of natural treatments, prescription medicines when needed and, most important of all, faith in the power of prayer and the ability to be led by the Holy Spirit whom Jesus said was the One who would guide each of us (and that includes doctors) to all truth. "Howbeit when he, the Spirit of truth, is come, he will guide you into all truth: for he shall not speak of himself; but whatsoever he shall hear, that shall he speak: and he will show you things to come" (John 16:13 KJV).

THE HEALING POWER OF NUTRITION

The foods we eat have a dramatic impact on our health. Immediately after God entered a healing covenant with man in Exodus 15:26, He began describing what man was to eat, how he was to prepare food, and so on (see Ex. 16). In Leviticus 11 and Deuteronomy 14, God outlined specific nutritional and health laws for man. We should not be amazed, therefore, that six of the ten leading causes of death in this country today are directly linked to our nutritional intake, and this includes diseases such as cardiovascular disease (heart disease and stroke), cancer, lung disease, pneumonia, and diabetes.

Food is a big business, with billions spent each year on eating out at every conceivable kind of restaurant—fast food, ethnic food, gourmet food, home-style food, carryout food, pizza, burgers, fish, and steaks. At the same time, Americans spend more on diet plans, weight reduction programs, pills, shots, and exercise equipment than the entire national budget of many countries. Isn't it ironic that Americans in reality are malnourished, overfed, obese, and nutrient starved? Many Americans have the same nutritional problems as people in Third World countries, but to the opposite extreme!

Nutritionists long ago discovered that the people living around the Mediterranean Sea had a lower incidence of the ailments and killer diseases that plague other populations. In fact, the lowest rate of heart disease recorded anywhere in the world was in the Mediterranean area, on the island of Crete. Amazingly, their diets contained almost the same amount of fat as we consume in the typical American diet, but it is a totally different fat, derived from olive oil and, to a lesser extent, fish. This monounsaturated oil actually prevents cancer, raises the level of good cholesterol, and lowers the rate of heart disease. They do eat some meat and fish as well as cheese and yogurt, but these are simply condiments that they add to their main meal portions, which are vegetables, legumes, fresh fruit, nuts, garlic, and tomatoes, as well as dark, crusty breads, cereals, pasta, and dark rice.

The Mediterranean-style diet has proved to have significant health benefits, including a role in reducing cholesterol and preventing heart disease. With its emphasis on foods traditionally known for being good sources of fiber and antioxidants, the diet also appears to lower the risk of cancer.[12]

A major medical trial, the Lyon Diet Heart Study, was designed to test the effects of putting people at high risk of heart disease on a Mediterranean type of diet to see if it would help prevent heart attacks. The study involved some 605 patients who had documented heart disease and had survived a heart attack.

Researchers discovered that the rate of heart attacks began to go down after only a *few weeks* on the diet. After two years, there was an astounding 76 percent reduction in the number of new manifestations of heart disease in those on the Mediterranean diet compared with a comparable control group. The blood levels of the antioxidants were higher, and the lipid profile was much better.[13]

The results of this study, which emphasized scientific insights into the heart protective effects of certain nutrients, were published by the *Journal of the American College of Cardiology* as well as by the prestigious British journal, *The Lancet.*

The bottom line is that it really does matter what you eat. God did not allow the first chapter of Genesis to end before He began talking about the food man was to eat (see Gen. 1:29). God later modified His eating plan in Genesis 9:3 (after the Flood), which, incidentally, is the plan followed by people all over the world today. The ideal diet seems to be the Mediterranean diet, adapted to various food availability in specific cultures and locales. We recommend it not only for its protection from heart disease, but also as protection from cancer. Yet it also seems to provide an excellent program of weight control and weight loss. We have actually had patients lose up to seventy pounds on the Mediterranean-style diet we utilize.

As you begin practicing *healing prayer* for yourself, a family member, or a loved one, God will lead many of you to seek out His natural health laws, the bulk of which are centered around nutrition. Other natural substances such as herbs may also be part of your unique pathway that will lead to your manifestation of healing. I encourage you to be open to God in these areas. Many people are healed, but they go back to the same destructive lifestyle that led to the disease in the first place. The disease comes back, and they even begin questioning God as a healer when, in reality, they did not maintain their healing because they were not aware of His divine laws of health. Yes, there is, in fact, a specific supernatural way to pray about various diseases, but this must always be combined with taking care of our natural bodies. The Bible says the treasure we have is contained in an earthen vessel (see 2 Cor. 4:7). Guard your earthen vessel so that you will fulfill God's promise in Psalm 91—that with long life you *will* be satisfied.

3

WHAT THE BIBLE SAYS
ABOUT HEALTH

I did my premed studies at Baylor University, the largest Baptist institution of higher learning in the world. So in addition to the concentrated emphasis on biology, chemistry, and vertebrate anatomy, there were lots of religion courses. One course took me back to the Old Testament. Another to the New Testament. And yet another required attending chapel twice a week. At the time, I thought, *I don't have time for this. I need to be studying for medical school.*

I just didn't see the relevance of these topics to my becoming a doctor and tended to regard them as nuisances. I fell prey to the commonly accepted misconception that there was no significant connection between religion and science in the treatment of sickness and disease in the human body.

Years later as I concentrated on my chosen area of specialty, preventive medicine, I found myself taking special note of the critical importance of diet, nutrition, exercise, rest, and hygiene to human health and wellness. Although some of the medical studies that validated these recommended practices had been done fairly recently, reading their conclusions gave me a strong sense of déjà vu—I'd seen that information somewhere before.

I soon rediscovered the source of a comprehensive code

of practical behavior that encompassed a large majority of practices and recommendations currently endorsed by modern medicine. Where? In the Old Testament! As Dr. S. I. McMillen noted in his very popular book, *None of These Diseases*, the Bible's sacred writings predate modern medicine by four thousand years. Following its teachings, he declared, "prevents devastating disease and senseless suffering."[1]

Almost everyone is aware of the divine laws handed down to Moses that we call the Ten Commandments. These laws established the spiritual, moral, and legal values that governed the people of Israel for centuries, and that make up the backbone of Christian ethics and morality as well.

But the Mosaic Law ultimately included hundreds of prescribed prohibitions and practices. The first five books of the Old Testament, the Pentateuch, include detailed, specific instructions concerning agriculture, food, sex, personal hygiene, treatment of certain physical ailments, religious practices, civic and social responsibilities, charity, and other important subjects.

WHAT THE BIBLE IS ABOUT

Although a great many people assume that the Bible is strictly a religious book dealing exclusively with "spiritual" matters, even a casual study of the Scriptures reveals that they deal with man as a whole person—body, mind, and spirit. The biblical text is largely directed to nurturing, protecting, and guiding human beings to achieve their full potential in every area of their being.

For example, biblical scholars have determined that one out of three Old Testament laws dealt with issues of health.

Although the purpose of those laws may not have been fully understood at the time they were established, we now know that each was carefully designed to make a definite, positive contribution to man's well-being.

Nothing was left to chance. The law detailed which plants and animals could be used for food and which were never to be eaten. Animals like camels, rabbits, and pigs were forbidden. Modern science can easily explain the dangers of unrefrigerated pork (trichinosis). And I remember learning as a boy that wild rabbits often get diseased, and their infection can pass on to humans if the rabbits are eaten (tularemia). I'm not sure about camels, but I've never had any desire to eat one.

Other animals forbidden as food included insects, vultures, buzzards, owls, bats, and several other kinds of flying creatures. Today's health scientists can explain why each creature could have adverse effects on anyone using them for food.

Other laws related to personal hygiene. These rules covered washing of bodies and clothing, proper disposal of human wastes, inspection and isolation of certain diseases (such as leprosy), and purification instructions for several different contaminations. Circumcision, once thought to be solely a religious practice, decreases genital cancer according to modern studies.

Thirty-five centuries later, medical science has confirmed the importance of each of these measures to public health. For example, instituting the simple practice of frequent hand-washing by attendants to mothers giving birth dramatically reduced the death rate of both mothers and babies. The use of quarantines to isolate patients with infectious diseases from the general population has saved untold millions of lives. No one had heard of such a practice until God revealed it to His people.

The Bible's laws related to sexual practices were much more than arbitrary moral codes. They were designed to protect people from the now-proven evils of family inbreeding, from the venereal diseases associated with adultery and prostitution, and from the mental and emotional sufferings of homosexuality.

The Mosaic Law also included instructions on how to care for the land. For six years out of seven, crops could be cultivated, vineyards grown, orchards harvested. But during the seventh year, the land was to lie fallow, to rest, to be replenished. Is it coincidence that students of modern agriculture now recommend crop rotation or allowing fields to lie fallow as a means of keeping soil vitamin and mineral levels high?

Solomon, acclaimed as the wisest man who ever lived, said, "The teaching of the wise is a fountain of life, turning a man from the snares of death. Good understanding wins favor, but the way of the unfaithful is hard" (Prov. 13:14–15 NIV).

As a physician, I am keenly aware of how much sickness is caused by improper care of the body. The laws of nature are God's laws for physical health and cannot be broken without consequence. One of my favorite Bible verses warns that "the curse causeless shall not come" (Prov. 26:2 KJV). Another way to interpret this is the curse (of disease) does not come without a cause. Physical healing—whether through natural or supernatural means—was never intended to take the place of proper care of the body through exercise, rest, proper nutrition, and avoiding damaging habits. Stopping disease before it starts is much more effective and beneficial than seeking to recover from sickness and repair the body from the ravages of disease.

Overeating plays a role in many modern-day diseases and ailments. Organs do not function well when the body is overnourished, obese, and overloaded. Or if the wrong kinds of foods are eaten, the body may not receive the essential nutrients for good health. The immune system can be damaged. Hardening of the arteries begins to take its toll.

Then there are those who injure their bodies through damaging habits. Chronic stress and sleep deprivation weaken our lymphocytes—the frontline warriors of the immune system. Substance abuse further weakens our abilities to fight off the attacks of disease.

THE IMPORTANCE OF WHAT YOU EAT

I believe a crucial key to healing and health is one's diet. What you eat, good or bad, to a significant extent determines the ultimate state of your health and well-being. As I mentioned previously, six of the ten leading causes of death in the United States have proven links to diet and nutrition. Heart disease, cancer, stroke, lung diseases, pneumonia, and diabetes are all impacted by the kinds and quantities of food we eat.

After years of studying the human body from the standpoint of finding ways to avoid sickness and prevent disease, I am convinced that our choice of foods—what we eat and what we avoid—is the most potent program for good health that is within our control. Further, I believe the dietary laws of the Bible offer solid guidance and valuable suggestions for us today.

As if to stress the priority and importance of a proper diet, the very first chapter of the Bible includes a specific description of what man should eat. It's not complex or difficult at all. "I give you every seed-bearing plant on the face of the whole earth and every tree that has fruit with seed in it. They will be yours for food" (Gen. 1:29 NIV).

A few chapters later, this vegetarian regimen was modified to include the flesh of some animals: "Everything that lives and moves will be food for you. Just as I gave you the green plants, I now give you everything" (Gen. 9:3 NIV). Basically, God's health plan includes eating fruits, vegetables, seeds, grains, and small amounts of animal substances.

This simple principle from Genesis 9:3 is validated by the diets of diverse cultures around the world. The only single plant containing complete protein is the soybean. Without eating soy products, you would have to carefully combine certain plant products and eat them consistently and in large quantities. This is why God gave us Genesis 9:3—the addition of certain animal products—to ensure that people would obtain adequate, complete, concentrated proteins in their diets.

In Mexico, a diet of tortillas and beans supplies protein, but Mexicans traditionally add small amounts of a meat such as poultry to ensure complete protein. In Puerto Rico, the principal meal is rice and beans (*arroz con gondules*); in India, it is rice and lentils (*kitcheri*); and in Italy, rice and peas are the staples (*risi e bisi*). But each of these diverse groups of people adds some meat to their diets—usually fish or chicken, and in some countries beef. In each case, the meat is often a condiment either added to other dishes or eaten in small quantities. God's original nutrition plan, written thirty-five centuries ago, is still being followed by people throughout the world.

God's health plan also includes a couple of "thou shalt nots"—don't *eat* fat and don't *be* fat. "This is a lasting ordinance for the generations to come," said the law. "You must not eat any fat or any blood" (Lev. 3:17 NIV). We are also to avoid obesity: "But take heed to yourselves and be on your guard, lest your hearts be overburdened and depressed (weighed down) with the giddiness and headache and nausea of self-indulgence, drunkenness, and worldly worries" (Luke 21:34 AMPLIFIED).

Significantly, from the first to the last chapter of the Bible, the Scriptures emphasize the health benefits of plants. We've already looked at Genesis 1:29 with its endorsement of seed-bearing herbs and fruits. Revelation 22:2 (KJV) says, "In the midst of the street of it, and on either side of the river, was there the tree of life, which bare twelve manner of fruits, and yielded her fruit every month: and the leaves of the tree were for the healing of the nations."

AN ANCIENT CASE STUDY

The book of Daniel reports a dramatic test of God's health food plan against a Babylonian diet of wine and "rich dainties." Nebuchadnezzar's army had conquered the kingdom of Judah and carried away many of the people as prisoners. The king ordered some of the brightest and best young men to be brought to him to learn the language and be trained to serve in his palace. They were to be fed the sumptuous fare from the king's own table, with an abundance of fat-laden, unhealthy foods.

Daniel, along with Shadrach, Meshach, and Abednego, asked to be excused from partaking of the rich food and wine and allowed to consume a diet of vegetables and water. The king's steward was reluctant to consent, afraid he would be punished if they were not as healthy as the other captives. Daniel persuaded him to test them for ten days and then see how their condition compared with the others.

At the end of the ten-day test, Daniel and his friends looked better and were healthier than the young men who ate the king's food. So they were allowed to continue their vegetables-and-water diet. At the end of the training period, the healthy eaters were strong and fit as well as clearheaded and keen of mind (see Dan. 1). What a great example of the benefits of a carbohydrate-rich diet (the carbohydrates being vegetables and fiber).

FOODS SPECIFICALLY MENTIONED IN THE BIBLE

The Bible specifically mentions many different foods that were used by people in Old Testament times. Basically, these foods are among those approved by the Mosaic dietary laws, and many have qualities that help both to prevent and to cure diseases. Most of the foods are still in use today and make up the diet of people living in the regions around the Mediterranean Sea. They include:

- *Meat*, without blood or fat, from animals with divided hooves, or animals that are cud-chewing, such as beef or veal, goat, lamb, venison, quail, partridge, game birds, and other poultry (Gen. 9:3; Lev. 7:22–27; 11:2–3).
- *Fish* with scales (Lev. 11:9; Deut. 14:9).
- *Olive oil* (2 Kings 18:32).

- *Vegetables* such as beans, cucumbers, garlic, leeks, lentils, olives, and onions (Num. 11:5; Ezek. 4:9).
- *Fruits* such as apples, figs, grapes, melons, pomegranates, raisins, and wine (Deut. 8:7–9; Song 2:5; John 15; Num. 11:5).
- *Grains* such as barley, millet, spelt, and wheat (Ezek. 4:9).
- *Dairy products*, including butter, cheese, curds, yogurt, eggs, and the milk of cows, sheep, and goats (Isa. 7:15, 22; Prov. 27:27).
- *Honey, pistachio nuts*, and *almonds* (Gen. 43:11).
- *Bread* (Ezek. 4:9).
- *Condiments* and *spices*, such as anise, bitter herbs, caraway, coriander, cumin, mint, mustard, rue, salt, wine vinegar (Matt. 23:23; Luke 11:42; Num. 11:7).

These foods have come to be referred to as the Mediterranean diet. I consider this basic diet of the ancient Hebrews to be the ideal eating plan for health. A typical day's meals might include dark bread or cereal, a piece of fresh fruit, and perhaps yogurt or cheese for breakfast. Lunch or dinner would likely include salad, soup, pasta, rice, and the staple vegetables and fruits, especially tomatoes, onions, and peppers. A small portion of meat or fish might also be included.

My wife, Linda, and I personally use a variation of the Mediterranean diet for our daily menu. I also recommend it to my patients as one of the best balanced and beneficial diets available, and we regularly receive testimonials of dramatic health improvements from people who try it.

"Today, it has been scientifically proved that the traditional Mediterranean food is healthy," according to a report from a French health agency. "Even nutritionists praise the Mediterranean diet as a healthy way of eating."[2]

Dr. Alexander Leaf of Harvard Medical School in Boston comments on several studies on the diet, noting that "relatively simple dietary changes . . . achieved greater reductions in risk [for heart attacks and strokes] than any of the (drug-oriented) cholesterol-lowering studies to date."[3]

Numerous scientific studies have found that populations whose diet is rich in seed foods such as maize, beans, and rice have significantly fewer incidents of major cancers, such as prostate, breast, and colon cancers, as well as coronary heart disease. In Houston, Texas, where I practice, a renowned cancer center did a research project that indicated that the protein from certain vegetable sources in seeds inhibited the formation of tumors. The published report of the study concluded that a prudent diet would derive one-third to one-half of all protein from seeds— exactly what Genesis prescribes!

As a Christian believer and a medical doctor, I am convinced that modern man can derive much benefit from the health laws and moral directives of the Bible. Every single thing we are discovering in science today parallels and bolsters what the Bible says about nutrition. Science is "walking in the footsteps of God."

When I was in premed, I was astonished that the dietary laws given in the ancient biblical texts revealed truths that scientists were only beginning to uncover in my day. After decades of intensive personal research, I believe more than ever that even with the amazing medical advances of our times, science is still in the position of "catching up" with the ancient laws God gave His people thirty-five centuries ago in the Bible. They are still for us today.

4

Do You Know How to Pray?

In Chapter 3 we discussed how the Bible is a reliable guide to nutritional practices that are ideally suited to man's physical health today. In this chapter we'll look to the Bible to see if it sheds the same light on definitive, specific prayer that produces results—healing and health for our bodies.

In his poem "Morte d'Arthur," England's Alfred, Lord Tennyson has King Arthur exclaim:

More things are wrought by prayer
Than this world dreams of. Wherefore, let thy voice
Rise like a fountain for me night and day.

"Prayer accomplishes more than you can imagine," he was saying, "so don't ever stop praying for me!"

What do you know about prayer? Do you believe in its effectiveness? How often do you pray in private devotional times and during your regular daily activities? Are you comfortable enough to pray aloud in small groups or public gatherings?

One more question: Where do you turn to find answers to your questions about prayer? Although I recognize that we live in a pluralistic society with many different religions and traditions, as a Christian I believe that only the Bible gives the definitive blueprint of how we should walk into the spiritual realm. There are hundreds of Scripture references about prayer and praying in both the Old and New Testaments that explain this intimate communion between the spirit of man and his Creator.

The bottom-line truth is that if you aren't already a prayer, there will come a time in your life when you'll need to know how to pray. Ephesians 6 talks about "the evil day." We all will face at some point a midnight hour. Malcolm Boyd, a theologian, wrote a best-selling book of prayers entitled, *Are You Running With Me, Jesus?* In the introduction, he related how he never ceased to be shocked by the many naive and superstitious misconceptions about prayer.

"On one occasion," he said, "a forty-year-old man, an intellectual and cultural leader, confessed that he had stood in agony at his young son's grave, unable to pray because he did not know the words of a single prayer."[1]

What a heartbreaking story! How sad not to be able to communicate with God at such a crucial hour because of the mistaken belief that the only language He understands is a memorized form.

LEARNING TO PRAY

Oral Roberts, a world-famous evangelist and founder of the university that bears his name, described how he learned to pray.

When I was a child, I would hear my parents talking to God as if He lived at our house. They were so natural about it. Sometimes they said just one word—"Jesus." Other times

they prayed a dozen words, or a hundred. I couldn't understand this for a long time. Then when I was dying with tu-
berculosis, my mother said to me, "You must pray, son."

I told her I couldn't . . . that I didn't know how to pray. I
remember her reply so well. She said, "Oral, you don't have
to know *how* to pray. Just talk to God. Just tell Him how you
feel."

So I began to do this, and as I talked to God He became
real to me too. I came to recognize Him as the Source for my
life and my healing.[2]

The Gospels relate that the followers of Jesus, after ob-
serving Him in prayer, came and requested that He teach
them to pray. He immediately gave them some simple instructions and a model prayer that is universally known as
the Lord's Prayer. It really should be called the *disciples'*
prayer since it was provided for their instruction.

I believe Jesus gave this prayer to the disciples not for
them to memorize and recite, but to teach them the principles of praying. It embodies certain fundamentals that all of
us should understand and apply to our prayers.

"Our Father which art in heaven, Hallowed be thy name."
We begin by acknowledging God as our Father, who is
therefore interested in our welfare and is approachable at
any time. As the chief resident of heaven, He is powerful,
deserving of our respect and devotion.

*"Thy kingdom come. Thy will be done in earth, as it is in
heaven."* As the ultimate "higher power," God's kingdom
precedes all earthly governments, and the working of His
will—which is *always* good—in our lives is greatly to be de-
sired.

"Give us this day our daily bread." God is our Source for

all the nourishment and nurture of our lives, and we should ask Him specifically to provide for our needs. This includes healing and health for every part of our beings.

"And forgive us our debts [transgressions, trespasses], *as we forgive our debtors."* God's perfection is greater than our imperfections, His wisdom far exceeds ours, and His divine mercy and grace are able to save to the uttermost when we seek forgiveness for our sins. But we are forgiven only when, and to the same degree that, we forgive others!

"And lead us not into temptation, but deliver us from evil." There is evil as well as good in the world, and we are imperfect. Only with God's active help can we overcome the pitfalls, problems, and opposition that we inevitably must confront in life.

"For thine is the kingdom, and the power, and the glory, for ever. Amen" (Matt. 6:9–13 KJV). Our success in prayer and in living requires us to understand and remember who God is and our relationship to Him.

With the guidance of Jesus' example, understanding how to pray seems much less confusing and mysterious, doesn't it? But imagine how puzzling and difficult it would be to learn how to communicate with God without the direction of His Word. That's why I say the Bible is essential to our spiritual development and is our road map and guide into the spiritual realm.

CAN WE TRUST THE BIBLE?

How can we be sure that what the Bible says is really true? Isn't it just another book of religious theories and rituals? What gives it such a high level of credibility? Without going into all the religious and theological arguments or examining the studies of language scholars and the intricacies of "higher criticisms," there are two major reasons I believe the Bible:

The first is because of faith. What I read in the Word of God transcends and goes beyond what I see, what I feel, and what I have experienced. The Bible speaks to something deep within me that I cannot articulate or even fully understand. But it resonates and rings true with every fiber of my being. In the words of an old Arkansas preacher, "I jus' *know* in my 'knower'!"

The second reason I trust the Bible is because I am a man trained in medical science and have seen its reliability in numerous areas confirmed by empirical evidence, historical cross-references, and scientific studies. For example, I've already related how the dietary laws of the Old Testament are constantly being confirmed by modern medical tests as the healthiest diet we can follow. The Mediterranean diet—which is essentially what the ancient Israelites ate—includes foods that science has now proved can actually help prevent and cure man's deadliest diseases.

I've also been intrigued by other objective findings by scientific disciplines that reinforce the truth of the Scriptures. Early secular histories, such as that of Josephus, attest to the accuracy of New Testament references to certain people and events. Anyone who has ever traveled to Israel and the Holy Lands has observed numerous sites of archaeological digs. The scientists involved in these excavations have found villages, cities, walls, fortifications, rivers, and springs exactly where the Bible said they would be, and exactly as the Old Testament described them.

Tablets, inscriptions, and pottery found in digs "shed new

light on interpretations of the Bible . . . Archaeology has confirmed and in fact expanded on many areas of biblical history," according to the Reader's Digest *Atlas of the Bible:*

> The essential facts of the Exile of the Jews in the 6th century B.C. have been confirmed; archaeologists have found evidence of the destruction and depopulation of virtually every site in Judah during this period. The wealth and power of Israel in Solomon's time, long thought by some to be exaggerated in the Bible, have not only been confirmed but may actually have exceeded the descriptions in 1 Kings and 2 Chronicles . . . As a consequence of these and many other discoveries, scholars have gained new respect for the biblical chroniclers.[3]

I've been told that during Israel's war of independence in 1948, in which the tiny, new nation was attacked by all the surrounding Arab states, its defenders turned to the Old Testament for insight into geography and historic battle strategies employed over the same Palestinian terrain centuries before. After fifteen months of fierce conflict, this poorly equipped, barely trained army prevailed over larger and stronger forces, successfully defending Israel's right to exist as a nation.

For these and many other reasons, I passionately believe in the accuracy and truth of the Bible. I have personally trusted and put to the test the teachings and promises of the Word of God. Over the years I have proved them again and again in my own life and experience, as well as with individual patients in my medical practice.

TRIED AND PROVEN RESULTS

We know that prayer works—it definitely gets results. Prayer changes things. Man has known it for centuries. Poets write about it. People from all walks of life testify to what they have experienced. And the positive effect of prayer in bringing healing to people has been tried and proved by scientifically controlled tests—thousands of them over the years.

Dr. Randolph Byrd, who was my classmate in premed, conducted one of the most famous scientific studies of the positive effects of intercessory prayer on patients in the coronary care unit at San Francisco General Hospital. He began his report on the results of the study with the rhetorical question, "Who has not, during a time of illness or pain, cried out to a higher being for help and healing?

"Praying for help and healing is a fundamental concept in practically all societies," he continued, "though the object to which these prayers are directed varies among the religions of the world. In western culture, the idea of praying for the benefit of others (intercessory prayer) to the Judeo-Christian God is widely accepted and practiced."[4]

In Byrd's study, he entered 393 patients into a double-blind randomized protocol, with 201 in a control group and 192 in an intercessory prayer group. The intercessors were "born-again" Christians active in daily devotional prayer and Christian fellowship with a local church. The results of the ten-month test were dramatic, with the patients receiving prayer having less congestive heart failure, requiring less diuretic and antibiotic therapy, having fewer episodes of pneumonia, fewer cardiac arrests, and being less frequently intubated and ventilated.

I found it interesting that at the end of Randy's paper, he acknowledged numerous people, some of them by name, who had helped with the project. At the end of that section he wrote, "In addition, I thank God for responding to the many prayers made on behalf of the patients."[5]

So the question is no longer *does* prayer work or get results, but *how* does it work. More accurately, what are the rules or guidelines for praying, especially for healing and health?

PRAYING BY THE RULES

There is order to all of God's creation, and so there is order to prayer. The guidelines for prayer are not nearly as complicated as some people try to make them. The first rule is to direct our prayer to the right place. Jesus said to pray to God the Father. He is the Creator of the universe, the Eternal One who has all power in heaven and earth, the Most High, the God of Abraham, Isaac, and Jacob. Finding Him is not really difficult because He wants to be found. The Bible says, "He that cometh to God must believe that he is, and that he is a rewarder of them that diligently seek him" (Heb. 11:6 KJV).

Paul, the great apostle, declared, "I know whom I have believed, and am persuaded that he is able to keep that which I have committed unto him against that day" (2 Tim. 1:12 KJV). Do you know the God you believe in? Without the inspired teaching of the Bible, we could be praying to almost anything—bugs, animals, statues and idols, unknown gods. Without biblical instruction, we could go about praying in entirely the wrong way. Instead, we can pray with confidence and assurance. Again, we are to pray to God our Father—in the name of Jesus.

There are several different kinds of prayers mentioned in the New Testament, each operating under certain conditions and guidelines. Some scholars have identified five to seven major kinds of prayer. Richard Foster speaks of more than twenty in his book *Prayer: Finding the Heart's True Home.* I've found at least ten or eleven distinct types of prayer in my studies, each with its own rules.

There is the *prayer of worship* that focuses on adoration and praise of God, not for what He has done or will do, but for who He is. There is united *prayer for the lost,* which does not seek the violation of any person's free will, but asks instead for continued expressions of God's love to the unsaved, for them to be convicted of their wrong ways, and for a harvester to cross their path and tell them of the good news of Jesus. The *prayer of commitment* requires the turning over of one's self and submitting one's will to God.

Other kinds of prayer include: *petition,* in which we acknowledge our dependence upon God and seek His help and provision for our personal needs; *intercession,* in which the needs and welfare of another individual are presented to the Lord; the *prayer of agreement,* in which two or more individuals believe together according to Matthew 18:19 for a specific petition; the *prayer of consecration and dedication,* the setting apart of individuals or physical things for service to God; the *prayer of binding and loosing,* which is a form of spiritual warfare; the *prayer of changing things,* which more often than not changes people as well; and the *prayer in tongues,* in which "the Spirit itself maketh intercession for us with groanings which cannot be uttered" (Rom. 8:26 KJV).

The Bible also speaks of an effectual, fervent prayer that avails much (see James 5:16). This is an intensive, dynamic, powerful manner of praying that continues to beseech God until the answer comes. This heartfelt crying-out mode can be employed in various kinds of prayer, especially the *prayer for healing*, which I believe should take an aggressive, detailed, positive form. I'll have much more to say about this kind of prayer later on.

Jesus made some dramatic statements about the power we have in prayer: "All things are possible to him that believeth" (Mark 9:23 KJV); and "Whatever you ask for in prayer, believe that you have received it, and it will be yours" (Mark 11:24 NIV). Can you imagine such things? All things are possible! Whatever you ask will be yours!

"This is the confidence we have in approaching God: that if we ask anything according to his will, he hears us. And if we know that he hears us—whatever we ask—we know that we have what we asked of him" (1 John 5:14–15 NIV).

Did you notice the conditions for receiving what you pray for? Believing, or active faith, and asking according to God's will. There's the catch, you say. What if I don't have enough faith? How do I know if what I'm asking is His will?

Let's deal with the faith issue first. The Bible says that everybody has faith. "God hath dealt to every man the measure of faith" (Rom. 12:3 KJV). So when God says to have faith and believe to get our prayers answered, it is reasonable, practical, and possible for us to meet that condition. God would not ask us to do what is beyond our ability.

The Bible also says that "faith cometh by hearing, and hearing by the word of God" (Rom. 10:17 KJV). Hearing the precepts and promises of the Bible proclaimed builds faith and enables belief. Attending church and Bible studies and reading or quoting key Scripture verses aloud get the Word of God in us and increase our faith.

There are times when we may not feel that our faith is very strong, or when doubt overshadows our belief. That's when we must realize that faith is not dependent on feelings, but the Word of God. God says it. We believe it. That settles it. One of the most honest prayers in the New Testament was prayed by a father who had brought his child to Jesus for healing. When the Lord told him that what he sought was possible if he could believe, the man cried, "Lord, I believe; help thou mine unbelief" (Mark 9:24 KJV). It has been my experience that when we do what we can do, then God will do what we can't do.

WHAT IS GOD'S WILL?

We've already seen God's promise that if we ask anything according to His will, He will hear us and grant our request. There are situations in which it is appropriate to ask for divine guidance and to pray, "If it be Your will." An individual considering a job change, a move to another city, or a decision to be a missionary to Africa might not know the best course and be uncertain of God's plan. Praying for God's will in such situations is right and proper, and will ultimately reveal the correct course of action and an accompanying sense of confidence.

On the other hand, we must not petition God for something that clearly opposes His plan and purpose, or that He has spoken against in His Word. There is little room for misunderstanding in the Ten Commandments, for example, so it would be ludicrous to seek God's will about whether it would be okay to lie, steal, kill, or commit adultery.

It is likewise wrong to say, "If it be Your will" when we pray for something He has already promised—like healing for our bodies! The Bible is full of promises and examples of God's direct, expressed will to heal us. Here are just a few examples from the King James Version:

I am the LORD that healeth thee. (Ex. 15:26)

[Jesus] healed all that were sick. (Matt. 8:16)

He sent his word, and healed them,
And delivered them from their destructions. (Ps. 107:20)

How God anointed Jesus of Nazareth with the Holy Ghost and with power: who went about doing good, and healing all that were oppressed of the devil; for God was with him. (Acts 10:38)

And the prayer of faith shall save the sick. (James 5:15)

What do these verses suggest to you about God's will concerning healing? Do you think that perhaps He has changed His mind since those statements were first made? The Bible says, "Jesus Christ the same yesterday, and to day, and for ever" (Heb. 13:8 KJV). If it was ever His will to heal, it still is today.

As I said in my book *The Bible Cure*, "The ministry of Jesus has, as a primary focus, the restoring of health to diseased bodies and tormented souls. Everywhere Jesus traveled in the Gospels, He acted like the Great Physician. In the four Gospels there are forty-one distinct accounts of physical and mental healing (with a total of seventy-two accounts in all, counting all duplications). In many stories, not just one person but multitudes were healed."[6]

One of my favorite stories from the Gospels is about a leper who came to Jesus and bowed down before Him. "Lord, if you are willing, you can make me clean," he cried (Matt. 8:2 NIV). There it is, the age-old question, "Is it God's will?"

How did Jesus answer? He reached out His hand and touched the man—the "unclean," the outcast. "'I am willing,' he said. 'Be clean!' Immediately he was cured of his leprosy" (Matt. 8:3 NIV). I don't see how there could be any clearer expression of God's will regarding healing.

DISCOVERING THE PATHWAY TO HEALING

I am a physician dedicated to helping people find health and wholeness. This I will do the rest of my days. My specialty is preventive and diagnostic medicine. I've always believed the best health plan for anyone is to never get sick in the first place. Preventive medicine means taking care of our bodies through proper diet, exercise, supplements, rest, and a wholesome lifestyle, as well as monitoring and treating any ongoing physical condition. Depending on each individual's environment, chemistry, and overall physical condition, the use of additional vitamins, herbs, minerals, and other nutritional supplements may be called for. Regular medical checkups are important to ensure that we are maintaining our health. They also alert us to the potential schemes or devices of the enemy.

As a diagnostician, through thorough physical examination and medical tests, I seek to find the root cause of my patients' problems and suffering. Then I help them devise a highly individual program of treatment and therapy that I call a *pathway to healing*. This pathway may sometimes use the best that medical science has to offer, including surgery, prescription medications, and physical therapy. It may use only natural herbs and supplements. It may involve strictly the spiritual approach, believing God for supernatural healing. All healing involves the supernatural since Jesus bore our infirmities on Calvary through His own blood. Frequently, however, a person's pathway to healing includes the supernatural power of prayer combined with the things we must do in the natural. Do not let these principles depart from you. They are critical to the health and healing of yourself, your loved ones, and all those hurting lives your path may cross.

When I am helping a patient to discover his or her own pathway to healing, I pray and seek God's wisdom and guidance. The Bible says, "But in everything by prayer and supplication, with thanksgiving, let your requests be made known to God" (Phil. 4:6 NKJV). I might pray, "Lord, You know all about Mrs. Jones's condition and what is needed to restore her body, mind, and spirit to complete wholeness. I thank You for sending Your healing power to her now. Reveal to us her pathway to healing. Show me the significance of these medical tests. Quicken my mind to know the appropriate medicines or natural therapies to combat the attack against her body and bring every cell, organ, and system back into balance and harmony. Direct me in ministering to her with every possible healing power, whether through prayer or medicine or natural means."

As I pray and open my heart and mind to the leading of the Holy Spirit, often a thought, idea, or impression will rise up inside of me. Sometimes it will be a question to ask the patient that may reveal additional needed information, or a confirming assurance that a certain medical treatment is the right course of action. Or I may have a strong impression to simply pray with the patient and wait for a period of time before doing anything else.

Whatever the case, I always make sure the patient feels peace with the course of action suggested and is in full agreement with it. After all, the pathway to healing we are seeking is for the patient and requires that person's full involvement, peace, conviction, and cooperation, with no reservation.

God's pathway to healing may be totally different for two patients with the same symptoms. I'll never forget one Sunday morning at church when I got a strong, urgent impression that I should approach a certain man and tell him to go seek a doctor for a checkup. He told me that he had never felt better and had been out doing hard work, pouring concrete, with no complaint. "Well, just pray about it," I said.

Not having a doctor, he asked if I would see him. We gave him a "stress test," monitoring his cardiovascular functions as he walked on a treadmill. In no time the readings were going off the chart, indicating probable artery blockage. "How do you feel?" I asked him.

"Terrific," he replied. "I could stay up here all day."

To make a long story short, further tests confirmed that the man had major, life-threatening plaque buildup in his arteries, restricting the flow of blood to his heart. Although he had never had any chest pain, shortness of breath, or other symptoms, he and I prayed together and God directed us to consult a specialist. Though the procedure is far overdone, God specifically directed him to undergo open-heart bypass surgery. His heart was a time bomb getting ready to explode. He went through the operation with no difficulty and soon resumed his active, vigorous lifestyle.

Another man came to me with all the classic symptoms of cardiovascular disease. He had angina (chest pain), shortness of breath, and general weakness. His blood pressure was high, with elevated cholesterol and triglyceride levels. He seemed a candidate for bypass surgery, based on the severity of his tests. Even cardiologists were recommending it.

But as I prayed, I felt led to pray the prayer of healing for the patient, get him to make some dramatic lifestyle changes in terms of diet and exercise, and treat him with some natural treatments and some conventional medicines—but no surgery. This was at odds with other medical opinions, so I prayed about it again. I wanted to be sure about this one. I received the very same impression again.

When I told the man and his wife what I felt led to recommend, they both were almost in tears. "This is exactly what both of us felt should be done, Dr. Cherry," they said. "We didn't want you to think we were afraid to have the surgery if you recommended it."

We prayed together and sent the man home to follow the pathway to healing we knew the Lord had given us. Within months his symptoms went away and he was a different person. Subsequent checkups confirmed that his condition was improving, and he was able to function normally and in comfort.

I'll have more to say about the *pathway to healing* concept in a later chapter. It has become the foundation and primary principle of my medical practice and teaching ministry.

PRAYING FOR HEALING

God has invited us to pray about all our needs, anything that
concerns us. He has given us faith to believe for answers to
our prayers. He has made it abundantly clear that it is His
will to heal us. And He has promised that our praying will
get results. Jesus said, "Ask, and it shall be given you; seek,
and ye shall find; knock, and it shall be opened unto you:
for every one that asketh receiveth; and he that seeketh find-
eth; and to him that knocketh it shall be opened" (Matt.
7:7–8 KJV).

So what are we waiting for? Prayer should be our first re-
course, not our last resort!

Sometimes people ask, "Why should I have to ask God for
things if He is all-knowing and already is aware of my
needs?" Foster answers the question by saying simply that
"God likes to be asked. We like our children to ask us for
things that we already know they need because the very
asking enhances and deepens the relationship. P. T. Forsyth
notes, 'Love loves to be told what it knows already . . . It
wants to be asked for what it longs to give.'"[7] Prayer releases
our anointing or power to take our spiritual authority over
disease.

How do we pray for healing? Specifically instead of generally. For example, if I were sick and you were going to
pray for me, I wouldn't want you to say, "Oh, God, please
heal everybody who is sick today." The problem would not

be that I didn't want other sick people to get well; rather, I simply need a strong, directed prayer that releases healing power to overcome my particular attack.

I need a directed, faith-filled prayer to overcome my problem and restore my body. This is what I call "speaking to the mountain of disease" when you pray.

Jesus said, "If anyone says to this mountain, 'Go, throw yourself into the sea,' and does not doubt in his heart but believes that what he says will happen, it will be done for him" (Mark 11:23 NIV). So I believe when we pray for healing, we should speak to the specific mountain of sickness and command it to be gone. We have this authority as believers.

Suppose the person we are praying for has a blocked artery. We should speak directly to that mountain and command the blockage to be absorbed and disappear. "God, I pray that the plaque formation—this scheme and device of the enemy—be reversed, that the cholesterol be reabsorbed, and that no blood platelets stick or bind to the plaque in the artery walls and obstruct the flow of blood. Your Word says that life is in the blood, and I claim Your life to be present in this body right now."

Or suppose that a person was diagnosed as having an advanced stage of melanoma, a particularly virulent skin cancer that can spread rapidly throughout the body if not detected and treated. How would a person speak to this mountain specifically? He should pray:

Father, the work of darkness of melanoma has attacked my body. These cancerous cells have divided abnormally in my body and have spread to my lymph nodes and vital organs. I know that You, God, have created within my body an immune system with cells designed and created to attack and destroy these abnormal cells. Therefore, Father, in the name of Jesus, my petition and prayer is that my immune system be activated. Lord, I say to my immune system, "Rise up, attack any abnormal cells, and rid my entire body of this melanoma." In addition, Father, I ask that the Holy Spirit continue to guide me to everything I need to do in the natural to enhance and strengthen my immune system.[8]

So many times I have seen what medicine calls "spontaneous remission"—I call it a healing by the power of God—occur when a patient speaks to a specific mountain of disease. As we seek and follow God's pathway, we see healings that cannot be explained by medical science.

When you pray, be bold and assertive. Don't be apologetic or timid. Be as aggressive in your praying as you are in seeking medical treatment. Martin Luther, the great Protestant reformer, described how he prayed for his sick friend, Melanchthon, also a leader of the church: "I besought the Almighty with great vigor . . . quoting from Scripture all the promises I could remember, that prayers should be granted, and said that he must grant my prayer, if I was henceforth to put faith in his promises."[9]

Remember that you are not "bothering" God with your requests when you pray. Nothing is too great or too small to bring to Him. After all, He invites you to come to Him with your needs and cast your cares upon Him. The Amplified Bible's version of 1 Peter 5:7 says, "Casting the whole of your care [all your anxieties, all your worries, all your concerns, once and for all] on Him, for He cares for you affectionately and cares about you watchfully."

For more than fifty years, Oral Roberts has been known as a man of faith and prayer. He was a pioneer in seeking to merge the healing streams of prayer and medicine, personally praying for multiplied thousands of sick people over the years. He also built a large hospital complex in Tulsa, Oklahoma, called the City of Faith, which was staffed by Christian doctors, nurses, and staff who prayed with patients as well as treated them medically. He was years ahead of his time. What was regarded as a bit radical then is now being studied, taught, and practiced by physicians and institutions across the country.

Brother Roberts says that the best way to be sure your prayer is answered . . . is to pray!

> God challenges you to do unlimited asking. To the one in need of salvation, He says, "Him that cometh to me I will in no wise cast out" (John 6:37). To the one in need of healing, He says, "I will come and heal him" (Matt. 8:7). To the one tormented by fear or dogged by failure, He says, "Come unto me . . . and I will give you rest" (Matt. 11:28). To the one who is a slave to habit, He says, "If the Son therefore shall make you free, ye shall be free indeed" (John 8:36).

> Are you expecting an answer? If you expect the Lord to do wonderful things for you, He will. Believe it, and you will find, as I have, that prayer is one of the most wonderful experiences ever known.[10]

5

A Doctor Learns How to Pray for the Sick

I didn't learn to pray for my patients in medical school. At the time, the University of Texas Medical School at San Antonio was to me a pretty much God-free environment. The training I received there focused exclusively on the physical and mental aspects of man. The emphasis was on medicine as *science*—technical, factual, mechanical.

In fact, patients who exhibited overt religious tendencies were often viewed with suspicion and, in many cases, as having mental problems. For example, if Christian patients prayed out loud or used the terminology that God had spoken to them, we might well send them for a psychiatric consultation to be sure the person was not exhibiting early symptoms of schizophrenia or some other kind of delusional behavior.

So like many doctors-to-be in medical schools all over the world, I grew more academically and intellectually proud, more self-centered and cynical, and less tolerant of any spiritual influences. In my case, I also became a captive of my own driving ambition. I wanted prestige and wealth—to have my own prominent clinic, enjoy the respect of my colleagues, and make a lot of money.

I didn't start out that way. As a young boy, my burning desire was to become a doctor. I genuinely wanted to help sick people get well, and believed I could. Even before I knew there was a specialized field of preventive medicine, my desire was to find a way to stop disease before it started instead of just treating its victims.

SEEKING THE UNREACHABLE GOAL

Studying medicine seemed an impossible dream because my family could not afford to pay for me to attend college. In fact, I was the first person in my family ever to attend an institution of higher learning. Not being a talented athlete, I knew my only chance was to earn an academic scholarship by studying hard and earning top grades. Education became my passion.

For generations my family had lived in the mountains of western Arkansas. When I was about six years old, my father's job as a salesman required us to move to the capital city of Little Rock. From there we were transferred to Oklahoma City, then to the great state of Texas, where we remained and where I was educated. My parents did all they knew to do to make a good life for our family, and they always gave me encouragement and love.

The members of my family were honest, moral, respectable, hardworking folks. We occasionally went to Sunday services or attended summer vacation Bible school, but church and God were not the center of our lives.

From about the third or fourth grade on, I discovered a dynamic and intense young preacher on television named Billy Graham. I was drawn to him and his message that God cared about and took a personal interest in the needs and problems of individuals in our modern age. Being the student that I was, I got my notebook and took careful notes each time his program came on. I wrote down Mr. Graham's main points and the Scriptures he quoted. Then I'd study them and read my Bible regularly for weeks, fascinated and intensely interested although I wasn't quite sure why. Then my interest would fade away. My attraction to Billy Graham's crusade telecasts and straightforward presentation of the gospel was repeated numerous times over the years—later I even attended one of his crusades—but there was never any lasting change inside me.

This was the extent of my religious experience when I graduated from high school and was ready to go off to college. For years I had applied myself to my studies, hoping for a scholarship to attend college. I had checked out several Texas schools, but I was drawn most of all to Baylor University. In addition to being the largest Baptist university in the world with an extensive curriculum of religion and Bible courses, Baylor had a highly regarded premed program. It was the latter that got my attention.

Fortunately, Baylor awarded me a scholarship and gave me a chance. From day one I was keenly aware that I had to excel in my studies if I was to have a chance to attend medical school. During the campus orientation, I sat with 1,500 other freshmen premed students as a professor said, "Look around at your fellow students. Four years from now only twenty of you will be going on to medical school." He went on to say that those who made it would be chosen on the basis of how hard they studied and how high their grade point average was.

I knew how to study. And I determined not only to make

it through premed and go on to medical school, but to be one of the elite group earning a scholarship. There was a lot of pride rising up in me.

THE SECULAR WAY TO STUDY SPIRITUAL THINGS

So my approach to all my classes—scientific and the required religious studies alike—was to get every answer right and make the highest possible grades on every test. Most of us premed students approached Bible study exactly as we would a physics or chemistry class. We virtually memorized the Old Testament. We knew all the genealogies, all the begets, and all the covenants. We didn't care about the spiritual foundations found in the biblical text. We regarded what was presented as information to be recalled for the tests.

Because the tests awarded extra points for correct answers on bonus questions, we premed students would sit in the back of the classroom and make bets with each other as to who would make the highest grade *above* 100 on the exams. Talk about pride. Talk about being driven.

In our New Testament classes, the professors talked about "the blood of Jesus," atonement, redemption, sanctification, justification, propitiation. We premed students dutifully wrote down each term and its definition in the exact same way we listed the biological names for the members of the plant and animal kingdoms or the anatomical labels for each part of the human body. We learned the material only long enough to pass final exams, considering religious information to be irrelevant to our chosen careers.

For some reason we didn't fully appreciate the opportunity we had to learn about the Bible and Christian theology from wise, dedicated men. Religion was simply part of the required core curriculum. So most of us never really tried to understand the deeper significance and meaning of the lessons.

My personal Christian knowledge was pretty limited. I believed Jesus Christ was the Son of God, knew the basic Sunday school stories, and from my limited television encounters with Billy Graham, had an image of God as loving, caring, and interested in man's present and eternal welfare. With such elementary knowledge and experience, I certainly could have benefited from a deeper understanding of the Scriptures and the basic principles of Christian faith.

But something happened that drove me even farther away from God rather than drawing me closer. In one of my New Testament classes, the instructor one day began talking on the subject of healing. Naturally, my ears perked up and the professor had my full attention.

What I heard stunned me at first, then made me angry and bitter. "Sickness and disease are tools God uses to teach people lessons," he said. "Sinful man tends to go his own way, ignoring God's plan for his life. So God sends pain and suffering to get his attention and make him turn back to the Lord. Or God may allow suffering to go on to make a person grow in patience and learn to trust and depend on Him. That may be why there is so much sickness!"

The idea of God wanting people to suffer—actually sending sickness upon them—was confusing to me. My dream, my goal, my whole life's purpose was dedicated to learning how to heal people, to help them get well and stay well. Indeed, I believed it was possible to find a way to help people never to get sick in the first place.

If my New Testament professor was right, my life's ambition was in direct opposition to God's will. I was setting out to fight God! I couldn't understand this at all. How could people be better off crippled and hurting, dying from cancer, heart disease, diabetes, and other terrible diseases? Why should they have to suffer physically to benefit spiritually?

If this was what real Christianity was about, I didn't want any part of it. If this was the true nature of God, I was, in essence, opposing Him by becoming a doctor. Unfortunately, not feeling qualified to challenge the professor's statements, I turned my back on spiritual matters and focused my attention exclusively on medical science.

Not surprisingly, like many other premed students, I came to resent the school's requirement that all first- and second-year students attend chapel for two hours each week. Rather than participate in the services and possibly find some level of spiritual enrichment, I went under duress, in frustrated aggravation, until I devised a plan to skip out without being caught. Believing there were more important things to do with my time, I devised a way to get someone to go to chapel in my place and sit in my seat. Now there was no chance of spiritual influence intruding into my secular studies.

MOVING ON TO MEDICAL SCHOOL

The main things I remember about my college years were class work and study halls. With no money for entertainment and little time to spare for socializing, my life was a spartan existence. Although I grew weary of the seemingly unending grind, I was afraid to let up. But my hard work paid off.

Because I was able to excel academically at Baylor, I applied to and was accepted by several medical schools after three years of premed instead of four. I chose to attend the University of Texas Medical School at San Antonio.

As I mentioned, it was probably the most godless environment I'd ever been in. By that I don't mean that the professors and students were evil, just that the total emphasis was humanistic. We were trained to consider only the physical and mental aspects of patients' health problems, with absolutely no thought of the spiritual dimension.

"If the patient's minister wants to pray, fine, as long as he stays out of the way of the real professionals," was the attitude. "Maybe he can offer some comfort and moral support. After all, if surgery, drugs, or other conventional therapies don't work, that's it. If medical science can't fix it, it can't be fixed."

By the time students became interns and residents, this attitude had become so ingrained that it sometimes had the effect of causing them to "dehumanize" patients and regard their work as a matter of conditioned responses. If you identify symptom A, use the blue pill; if you diagnose disease B, use an IV to inject 10 cc of drug C. And it was not unusual to overhear a discussion of "the gall bladder in 3108" instead of referring to the patient by name.

No doubt the pressure from the heavy caseloads found in teaching hospitals also contributed to this kind of behavior, but I believe much of it was a direct result of the "tunnel vision" focus on people as physical and mental case histories instead of complete individuals. For the most part, these new doctors had no intention of being deliberately callous or insensitive, and the overwhelming majority probably went on to become competent physicians.

I found the classroom work and study hours at medical school long and challenging, but at the same time intensely interesting. Without question, my lifelong ambition to become a doctor was right on target. I knew this was exactly what I was supposed to do. And I could hardly wait to complete medical school and start "hands-on" practice.

DR. KENNETH COOPER'S AEROBIC CENTER—MY FIRST JOB!

After being licensed to practice and completing my training, I stumbled across a unique opportunity. I met Dr. Kenneth Cooper, a brilliant and innovative doctor who had created a simply structured exercise and total fitness program he called *Aerobics*, described in a popular book that had sold more than six million copies. He operated one of the country's most elite clinics, The Aerobics Center/Cooper Clinic in Dallas, specializing in the then-unusual specialty of preventive medicine.

Fascinated to discover that someone was actually doing what I had dreamed about even before I went to medical school, I blurted out, "I would like to come work for you." It did not occur to me that he might not be interested in a twenty-six-year-old, fresh out of training, with little experience. I never stopped to think that older, more qualified doctors than me might already have applied for staff positions with Dr. Cooper.

As it happened, Dr. Cooper did have an immediate opening and urgently needed a physician to see previously scheduled patients. In a matter of days I had a formal interview and was hired. Was this all a dream? On my very first job I was practicing preventive medicine at a prestigious clinic, treating people with current medical conditions, but also helping them take preventive health measures through exercise, nutrition, and other significant lifestyle changes.

Within a matter of weeks new patients were calling and asking for appointments to see me because their friends had been seen by me. Then those new patients recommended me to others. Before long I started getting invitations to give speeches around the community and state about preventive medicine. And more patients called and asked for me by name. In a very short time I was making money in amounts I'd never dared to even dream about.

But I didn't handle success very well. My growing income, along with the gratifying response to my public appearances and the pride at being asked for by name at the famous Cooper Clinic, sent my ego soaring. Growing more cocky and self-centered by the day, in about a year my arrogance persuaded me that it was time for me to go out on my own.

"I appreciate what you've done for me, Dr. Cooper," I told my mentor, "but it's time for me to be moving on."

"I think that would be a mistake, Reg," he replied. "You're not ready to make it on your own yet. I'd like for you to stay."

In my incredible brashness, I—a twenty-something nobody, an insignificant doctor whose only success had come through the world's leading figure in preventive medicine— declared, "Well, Dallas is just not big enough for the both of us! I'm going to start my own preventive medical practice in Houston."

What could anybody say in response to such foolish ignorance? So that strong, decent Christian doctor said good-bye and watched me walk away.

DOING MY OWN THING

The first year on my own was brutal. I nearly starved to death. My new clinic was in the far northern suburbs of Houston, and very few people were willing to drive out into Montgomery County to see a beginner doctor practicing some newfangled specialty they'd never heard of before. And as Dr. Cooper had predicted, I was struggling.

I decided to move to the middle of Houston and start over where there might be more prospective patients. I might not have made it there either, except Dr. Cooper's status propped me up again. A reporter for the *Houston Post* discovered that I had worked for the Aerobics Center and came out to interview me for an article on preventive medicine, which was so new at the time that I was its only practitioner in Houston.

Largely as a result of that article, people learned about my practice and started scheduling appointments. My practice started growing and getting established. Soon large companies began signing up their employees to come through the clinic for diagnostic and physical exams. Important executives and wealthy professionals from Houston and many other areas began seeking me out for physicals and preventive medical programs. In a relatively short time my new clinic got very busy.

At first I tried to handle all the patient exams and direct medical care myself, in addition to supervising my growing staff, reviewing medical records, managing the business functions such as insurance filing and billing, and trying to stay current with my reading in the medical journals. I was so motivated and ambitious that I thought I could do it all. But the practice and the workload kept growing. After unending months of twelve- and fourteen-hour days, I had to admit that even I could not handle it all by myself.

So I moved my offices to a larger facility and hired two more doctors and the supporting staff they needed to handle the increasing patient load. In no time the new office was packed, scheduled full all the time. As a result, I soon had a larger income than I'd ever thought possible.

I was getting more and more calls to speak about preventive medicine. Large corporations and professional groups wanted to know how they could help their employees prevent heart disease, cancer, and other stress-related illnesses. Getting the invitations and being introduced as an authority on medicine's newest specialty enlarged my ego even more.

In addition to speaking around Houston, I was flown to Lake Tahoe, to Florida, and all over the country to speak to conferences and conventions. I was also asked to write articles for various magazines, journals, and medical publications. I was being billed as one of medicine's rising young stars. It was heady stuff.

At the age of twenty-eight, money, recognition, power, and prestige were all coming my way. But instead of being thankful for my good fortune, I became egotistical, overbearing, and arrogant.

Having come from a family with very modest financial means, I thought money and an affluent lifestyle were the ticket to success. So I started spending money and accumulating things. I got expensive clothes and a sharp car—actually, a whole fleet of them. I bought a sedan, a sports car, a four-wheel-drive sports utility vehicle, and a pickup truck. I bought some property in the county where I lived and had several acres of land back in Arkansas where my family had previously lived. To develop and work on the property I owned, I even bought a bulldozer.

At first I enjoyed the "stuff" I was accumulating, but after a while these things failed to satisfy me. Wearing expensive clothes, driving a sports car, and eating in fancy restaurants weren't doing it for me. Pretty soon I was bored by it all.

I took up long-distance running, feeling that it offered the physical and mental challenge I needed. It became an obsession. I was so driven at everything I did, going all out, full steam ahead, that I decided to become a marathon runner. After a full morning of seeing patients, I'd take off to Houston's Memorial Park to run. Knowing that marathoners have to be able to run twenty-six and two-tenths miles, I ran around the jogging trail lap after lap, up to twenty miles at a time.

I enjoyed the camaraderie with other runners and the attention I got from people for my efforts, running in circles for hours. But it started losing its appeal fairly soon, especially after my knees became so sore and achy that I wondered if I'd ever be able to take another step again, much less to exercise or run.

THE MEANEST BOSS IN THE WORLD

I then turned all my attention back to my medical clinic. My practice was exploding! We saw a full schedule of patients every day, and had a waiting list. I also had a file of résumés from medical professionals who wanted to work for me. I began to push and drive my staff, including the other doctors, the nurses, the technicians, and the clerks. I pushed everyone, including myself, harder and faster.

I became a tyrant as a boss. If I felt someone wasn't trying hard enough or doing what I wanted, I'd fire them. Then
I'd pull out an application from the file and replace the person, often by the next day.

One day I came to work and didn't think my staff was
hustling enough. So I told a technician to go buy the sound-
track recordings of the themes from the movies *Rocky* and
Patton. "When I walk in here tomorrow, I want to hear that
music playing, and I want to see every staff member hustling. And keep those tapes playing all day!"

I developed the reputation of being the meanest boss
around. I never smiled when I was at the clinic. I was always dead serious. A raging drive and inner turmoil kept me
agitated and miserable. And I worked hard to be sure everyone around me felt the same way!

But no matter how hard I pushed to have the largest and
most successful medical practice, I was not satisfied. I had
the prestige, all the patients I wanted, a staff of seventeen
people, and all the things money could buy. But something
was missing in my life. I was miserable.

About this time a drama began to unfold in the life of one
of the nurses at the clinic. She had been through several bat-
tles and tragedies in her personal life, and she had felt the
pressure and frustration of the misery I'd inflicted upon the
staff at our clinic. Then everyone began to see a noticeable
change in her. Even I could see there was something different about her. The rumor was that she'd "found religion"
and become one of those Jesus people.

Unbeknownst to me, she had given her life to the Lord,
and had started praying for me. As mean as I was, she knew
I was miserable inside with an emptiness that only God
could fill. I found out later that she had requested prayer for

me at her church and even said to her Saturday night prayer group, "Please pray for my mean boss, Dr. Cherry. He needs help—he needs the Lord."

One day my car broke down, and I needed someone to drive me over to the repair shop. This nurse, Linda, agreed to take me. When we got to her car in the parking garage, I noticed a small Jesus sticker on the back bumper and just shook my head. When she started the car, the radio was playing music from a Christian station. "Do you play hymns all the time?" I asked.

"They're not really hymns," she said, "although I do listen to Christian music. But I'll turn it off."

As we rode along, I noticed that there was a new peace about Linda. She had more reason than I did to be frustrated and defeated by life, but she seemed serene. How different her life appeared to be from my own. She didn't say a lot to me—she didn't have to. I could see the change in her. And sensing her quiet assurance and composure, I was even more aware that I needed something more.

Linda and her church friends kept praying for me. And as I now know, when people start praying, something is going to happen. Events and circumstances start changing.

MY PERSONAL CONFRONTATION WITH GOD

In my case, for the first time in years I found myself thinking about God. I remembered seeing Billy Graham on television when I was young, and later attending one of his crusades and even going forward during the invitation. But the words I had prayed then were just from my lips, not my heart. I even thought back to my days at Baylor University when I'd studied terms like *redemption* and *sanctification.*

Days and weeks went by. At the strangest times I'd remember something with a spiritual connection, or I'd think about God for no apparent reason. At the same time I was growing increasingly uncomfortable and discontented with my life, crying out on the inside, yearning for something more, something better, a deeper reality than I had found.

One night in November 1979, God began to speak to me! No, I didn't hear an audible voice. I didn't have a dream or a vision. No ethereal being materialized and appeared to me. But I became distinctly aware of thoughts or impressions with complete and unmistakable clarity. I recognized it as that "still, small voice" Elijah heard in 1 Kings 19:12 and that Saul of Tarsus heard coming out of a light from heaven described in Acts 9:3–4.

God said to me, "I see your misery. I see your seeking. I know about your longings. I see you hungering for something in your life. The peace that you want I will give you. That longing in your heart I will satisfy. I will give you the desires of your heart. I will give you total joy and peace in your life."

I knew I was at a crossroads in my life. I couldn't go on living the way I was any longer. I had to either respond to the voice of God and turn my life over to Him, or turn my back and cast Him totally out of my mind. As I pondered this decision, I heard God's voice again.

"One thing I ask of you," He said. "You must give your whole life to Me—*everything* in your life. I'll give you joy unspeakable if you'll give it all to Me, everything you've got."

I did some more thinking. What was God asking of me? I

had a million-dollar medical practice, land, cars. Would I have to give up all these things to live for Him?

Then I heard the Voice say one final thing that left me breathless. "You have been to this point with Me before but never made a real commitment. This is the last time I'm going to bother you about serving Me." I felt an icy chill in the pit of my stomach, and I knew there was no tomorrow for my decision. I was facing my last opportunity, and I had to decide—right now!

So on that night in late November 1979, I thought it all over for the last time and made my decision *for Christ*. I said, "God, I have no idea what I'm doing, but"—and for the first time in years I said the name of Jesus. "Jesus, I'm sorry for the life I've lived. I give You everything I own, and I want to live for You the rest of my days. I give You my life."

At that instant I experienced what the apostle Paul wrote about: "Therefore, if anyone is in Christ, he is a new creation; the old has gone, the new has come!" (2 Cor. 5:17 NIV). Something inside me was totally different. I felt a joy I'd never known before. I truly was born again!

The next day I could hardly wait to tell Linda, the Christian nurse at the office, what had happened. I called her into my office before we started seeing patients. When she walked in, I had a big smile on my face, and I blurted out, "I found God!"

She was startled. "You did what?"

"I found God," I repeated.

"You mean you accepted Jesus as your Lord? You are born again?"

"Yes, yes, I did, I am!"

Even though she and her church friends had been praying for me, she could hardly believe what had happened.

That nurse who prayed for her mean boss was Linda, who is now my wife. She continued to be my nurse for years, part-time while we raised our two children. Linda and I now cohost our weekly television program, *The Doctor and the Word,* and she helps direct our ministry office.

LEARNING TO MINISTER TO THE SICK

Shortly after I accepted the Lord, we found it necessary to move our offices again to accommodate the new direction of our practice. As I was praying about the move, again the Lord spoke to me. He said, "I want you to practice the same kind of medicine, but I want you to establish a Christian clinic. From now on when you practice medicine, you are going to be ministering to patients. No longer will you address just the physical and mental aspects of the men and women that I will send to you. You must address the spiritual aspect also. This is the plan I want you and your patients to follow."

So when I started over with a new office in a new building, I also made some changes in my staff. Not everyone on the staff was comfortable or in agreement with the new direction of the practice. So I began to build my staff with Christian nurses and office personnel.

God changed our practice totally, empowering us to discern spiritual things and to minister to our patients spiritually as well as medically. We began to emphasize complementary medicine, combining prayer and spiritual counseling, conventional medical therapy, and many "alternative" remedies based on natural substances, including vitamins, minerals, herbs, and supplements.

For much too long there have been barriers between the various healing methods, which have had the effect of limiting the restorative benefits God has made available to us. We've already talked about how for centuries the medical profession focused only on the mental and physical aspects of the human body, treating symptoms and their underlying causes in much the same way a mechanic might repair a broken machine.

But many Christians who believed in and practiced spiritual healing were perhaps one-sided also, emphasizing only faith and prayer for the sick and ignoring anything in the natural. By seeking help only from supernatural means, they often overlooked other valid sources of healing, even from the Scriptures. The Bible's rich teachings on practical health issues such as diet and hygiene were largely ignored in the mistaken belief that the Old Testament has limited value for today.

At the same time, proponents of alternative medicine often have been antagonistic to both conventional medicine and spiritual healing. And to a large extent, until only recently, both the medical and spiritual camps have failed to take advantage of the tremendous store of natural substances with healing and preventive health qualities.

Rather than getting comprehensive, complementary, unified care, people with health problems must go to different places and different people, seeking to have all their needs met. A person might be prayed for by his pastor on Sunday and be treated with prescription drugs by his doctor on Monday. His spiritual leader might say, "You just have to have hope and faith," while his medical counselor says, "Just be patient and don't get your hopes too high." A well-meaning religious friend may suggest that perhaps God put this affliction on him to help him grow, while his doctor says, "Let's do all we can to get you free of disease."

If the patient happens to go into a health food store or reads a magazine or catalog about herbal remedies or natural treatments, he may hear extravagant claims that if he takes a particular vitamin, herb, or mineral, he won't need medicine, exercise, or diet.

GOD'S PATHWAY TO HEALING

No wonder people are so confused today, often losing confidence in all sources of healing therapy. That's why I believe God directed me to help people discover a personalized *pathway to healing* that is right for their individual needs rather than a one-size-fits-all approach.

In our clinic, we start with a detailed "head to toe" medical evaluation, checking every major system in the body instead of looking only at "the part that hurts." Once the tests are done, with prayer I review the findings and the medical history, seeking God's guidance and direction in determining the patient's needs. As I pray, the Lord gives me insight into the person's condition and a clear idea of a treatment approach.

When I meet with patients, I try to give them as much information as I can and find out their attitude and outlook toward their situation. I explain the concept of God's pathway to healing and seek their cooperation in discovering what their personal healing pathway should be. As we discuss their condition and lifestyle, a course of action begins to take shape.

Sometimes the pathway to healing is built around

conventional medical treatment, such as surgery, prescription drugs, and specialized physical therapy. I might also prescribe a weight loss program (if needed), an exercise program, detailed nutritional guidelines, and possibly recommendations for additional vitamins, minerals, herbs, and supplements. And I pray with the person, asking God to lead the patient into perfect health and wholeness, as He reveals to us each person's unique pathway to healing and health.

At other times I may feel directed to pray a healing prayer for the person as the primary and only therapy, always directing the patient to God's nutrition plan rather than prescribing drugs and medicines.

Whatever the situation, once we have found the personalized pathway to healing that God reveals for an individual, I counsel the patient on how to pray effectively for healing from the condition, giving the patient the details that will enable him or her to "speak to the mountain" in his or her unique situation.

We've seen some astounding things happen as we have practiced medicine that is bathed in prayer. We'll look at some specific case histories and the specific ways God instructed us to pray for particular conditions in a later chapter.

6

THE SIX BIBLICAL FOUNDATIONS FOR HEALING

In this chapter, the "rubber meets the road" with regard to healing. Step-by-step we will outline the six things you must know to see the manifestation of healing in your life and in the lives of those God calls you to pray for.

The Bible is a healing book. It teaches, without a doubt, that God wants you healed, that He has promised to take away sickness and disease and make you whole. From Genesis to Revelation—from the first chapter to the last—the Word of God talks about healing and health. It belongs to us.

If you study the life and ministry of Christ in the four Gospels, it's easy to see why He is known as the Great Physician. He seems to have devoted two-thirds of His public ministry to healing the sick. Wherever you find Jesus in the Bible, He is on His way to heal someone, He is on the scene bringing healing and deliverance, or He has just set the captive free and is on His way to help another.

F. F. Bosworth was an evangelist/teacher whose ministry began around the turn of the twentieth century, and he wrote the classic book *Christ the Healer*. He once said, "Instead of saying, 'Pray for me,' many people should first say, 'Teach me God's Word, so that I can intelligently co-operate with God for my recovery.'" This is excellent advice. Only God's Word gives us faith to believe God for our healing.

As a Christian physician, I am constantly amazed at how biblical wisdom and medical knowledge go hand in hand. The more we try to bring our everyday lifestyles into harmony with God's biblical plan, the closer we find ourselves following modern medicine's basic rules for healthy living. As I so often say, God's original plan was that man would never get sick in the first place. But when sickness and disease came into the world as a result of man's sin, God provided a way for mankind to be healed and restored.

While the Bible is filled with many examples and principles of healing, I want us to look in detail at six specific biblical foundations of healing. In no way am I suggesting that these are the only six truths of healing, but in my personal Christian experience and in my medical practice, I've found these biblical foundations to be the ones that get people healed.

1. GOD WANTS US TO BE HEALED

We must settle it once and for all: God wants us healed. Read these Scriptures from the Amplified Bible:

I am the Lord Who heals you. (Ex. 15:26)

I will take sickness from your midst. (Ex. 23:25)

And the Lord will take away from you all sickness. (Deut. 7:15)

He sends forth His word and heals them. (Ps. 107:20)

For I will restore health to you, and I will heal your wounds, says the Lord. (Jer. 30:17)

He . . . restored to health all who were sick. (Matt. 8:16)

They will lay their hands on the sick, and they will get well. (Mark 16:18)

By His wounds you have been healed. (1 Peter 2:24)

I could list dozens of additional verses, but you get the idea. God's desire for us is that we be healed, delivered, and made whole! I believe it is crucially important that you know and believe this with all your heart if you need healing. If you have any doubt at all, it can hinder your ability to get well.

The Bible says that Jesus "went about doing good, and healing all that were oppressed of the devil" (Acts 10:38 KJV). He came to "destroy the works of the devil" (1 John 3:8 KJV). Was it God's will for this to be done?

It must have been, because Jesus declared, "For I have come down from heaven not to do my will but to do the will of him who sent me" (John 6:38 NIV). He explained to His disciples, "Anyone who has seen me has seen the Father . . . it is the Father, living in me, who is doing his work" (John 14:9–10 NIV).

When Jesus Christ came in flesh to man, teaching about the kingdom of God, healing the sick, and forgiving sin, He was expressing the divine will of God. The Father in heaven was saying, "Hear this! I am speaking to you. When you see My Son, Jesus, you see Me. When you feel His power, you feel My power. He is the brightness of My glory, the express image of My personality. He is My Word to you."

Is it God's will to heal? Consider this. When Jesus taught His disciples to pray, as we've seen, He told them to ask that

God's will would be done on earth as it is in heaven. Would you expect to find sickness, disease, and suffering in heaven? Of course not! So if it is not God's will for people to be sick in heaven, how can anyone think it could be God's will for anyone to be sick on earth?

Beware of the "Wiles of the Devil"

Some people allow themselves to be deceived by Satan's sly suggestions that in some way God gets glory from their suffering. "If it's God's will, He'll heal me," they say resignedly. "If not, I'll just be patient and try to endure." And they go through life clinging to their sickness.

I heard about a woman who had suffered like this several years ago. She had been to many doctors and had had various treatments and taken much medicine, but was no better. Then she had gone to every minister and evangelist she had heard of who prayed for the sick, but she still didn't get healed.

Then she showed up at a camp-meeting revival, still sick and suffering. The evangelist was an old-fashioned faith preacher, and when he saw the woman, he asked if she wanted him to pray for her.

"I guess so," she said.

"Do you mean you aren't sure whether or not you want me to ask God to heal you?" he demanded.

"Well, I just don't know if it's His will for me or not," she whined. "I wouldn't want to displease God."

The evangelist got a little upset. "What kind of God do you think He is, anyway? Do you think He gets pleasure out of seeing you suffering and in pain?"

"Don't get mad at me," she said. "It just seems that if God

wanted me well, I'd get healed. Maybe I'm just supposed to endure this tribulation for the glory of God."

The minister thought about it for a minute. Then he said, "You know, maybe you're right. God probably does want you to be sick. After all, you make an awfully good patient, and you can probably endure a lot more pain before you die."

The woman gasped, completely shocked by what he was saying. And he didn't stop there.

"Tell me," he said, "are you still going to the doctor?"

"Yes."

"Well, stop going! Don't go back another time. And by the way, are you taking any medicine?"

"Oh, yes, lots of it."

"Then throw it all away. Don't go get another shot or take another pill."

The woman looked as if she was about to faint. When she could get her breath, she blurted out, "I can't do that, I'd die!"

The evangelist replied, "Well, God must want you dead. If it's not His will to heal you, then you certainly shouldn't do anything to prevent His will from being done. So don't even try to get well. Just stop everything and lie down and suffer until you die!"

That was pretty rough shock treatment. I don't know if I could be that blunt and abrupt in dealing with a patient. But I'm told that little woman sure changed her outlook about God's wanting her to be sick.

And just like that woman, you must make up your mind about whether or not God wants you to be healed. How many times have you been thrilled by the great stories of God's healing power in the Bible? Have you noticed in reading about the life of Jesus how much of His time He spent healing the sick? Do you personally know anybody who has been healed supernaturally by God's power?

Then hear the voice of God speaking to you: "I am the Lord, I change not" (Mal. 3:6 kjv). "Jesus Christ the same yesterday, and to day, and for ever" (Heb. 13:8 kjv). "God is no respecter of persons" (Acts 10:34 kjv).

If God ever healed anybody, then He will heal you. He has never been any better or more powerful than He is right now. God wants to heal you . . . now.

2. THE PRICE FOR OUR HEALING HAS ALREADY BEEN PAID

When Jesus came to earth, it was obvious that man had two tremendous needs. He was very sinful. And he suffered from all kinds of sickness and disease.

There had been a time when man didn't need anything. He didn't need forgiveness of his sin. He didn't need healing for his body. He didn't need food to eat or clothes to wear. He didn't need protection. He didn't need entertainment or fellowship.

Of course, I'm talking about those first wonderful days of time when the world was new. Adam and Eve lived in the Garden of Eden, an actual paradise filled with good things and the presence of God.

Then something happened that was to alter the course of world history until the end of time: sin came into the world. Adam and Eve disobeyed God. And from that moment, everything that had been all right was all wrong. All that had been perfect was now twisted and ruined.

Man's disobedience to God brought immediate consequences. His purity gone, man fell victim to sin. His divine health destroyed, he was susceptible to sickness. That day he began to die. A *double curse* had come upon man—sin and sickness.

Generation after generation of mankind was to experience the misery, heartache, and eternal penalty for sin. And generation after generation suffered the agony of affliction and pain of sickness and the awful terror of death.

Centuries rolled by, and still man was trapped and helpless in the deadly grip of sin and sickness. Then one day Christ stepped from His heavenly throne in glory. "It is enough," said the Father. "Go down and redeem the world from the double curse." So Jesus came down to bring the light and hope of salvation and healing—*a double cure for a double curse.*

Strange as it may seem, while all Christians believe that Christ died upon the cross to redeem mankind from sin, there are some who aren't sure about healing. They have never understood that on the same day Jesus was crucified, He also took upon Himself our sicknesses, supplying redemption for the body of man as well as for his soul.

If we believe in salvation—Christ's sacrifice on the cross to forgive our sins—then we must believe in healing because Christ also bore our sickness: "Himself took our infirmities, and bare our sicknesses" (Matt. 8:17 KJV). The price was paid for our healing as well as for our salvation.

Will You Receive What Jesus Has Provided?

The words *whosoever* and *whosoever will* are used in the Bible in giving an invitation to sinners to be set free from the penalty of sin. The words *as many, everyone, all,* and *any* are used to invite the sick and diseased to come and feel the healing touch of Jesus' hand of mercy. To those who answer the invitations, the results are always the same—salvation, healing, and new life.

Bible scholars have found a very powerful Greek word used in several places in the New Testament to describe the results of Christ's redemptive work. It is the word *sozo*. In Acts 2:21 (KJV), this word is translated "saved"—"whosoever shall call on the name of the Lord shall be *saved*." *Sozo* is also translated "saved" in Mark 16:16, Romans 10:9, and several other places.

Yet this same word, *sozo*, was also used to express what Jesus said to the leper—"thy faith hath made thee *whole*" (Luke 17:19 KJV). It is the same word used in Luke 8:36: "He that was possessed of the devils was *healed*" (KJV).

The psalmist David wrote, "Bless the LORD, O my soul, and forget not all his benefits: who forgiveth all thine iniquities; who healeth all thy diseases" (Ps. 103:2–3 KJV). David certainly included both salvation and healing in his praise to God.

Isaiah declared in prophecy, "But he was wounded for our transgressions, he was bruised for our iniquities: the chastisement of our peace was upon him; and with his stripes we are healed" (53:5 KJV). Again, obviously there is provision for deliverance from both sin and sickness.

When Jesus came and began to preach the gospel of the kingdom, He proved to be the Healer of sickness as well as the Forgiver of sin. The same Christ who said, "Arise, and take up thy bed" also said, "Son, thy sins be forgiven thee"— to the very same man (Mark 2:5, 11 KJV).

Jesus came against sickness and disease. He was deeply moved with compassion when He saw people who were afflicted and in pain. So great was His love that He identified with them in their suffering. He touched them and allowed them to touch Him. He placed healing within their reach.

I believe Jesus still heals today, in soul and body. The salvation of a suffering human soul is the greatest healing of all. And the healing of sickness and disease is included in the price Jesus paid.

James said, "And the prayer of faith shall save the sick, and the Lord shall raise him up; and if he have committed sins, they shall be forgiven him . . . Pray one for another, that ye may be healed" (James 5:15–16 KJV). This apostle recognized the truth that God wants to heal both of man's great needs.

If you need to be saved—forgiven of your sins—Jesus died for you.

If you need healing for some sickness or disease that has attacked your body, Jesus died for you.

His death on the cross brings healing and salvation, the answer to man's two greatest needs.

3. BE PERSISTENT IN SEEKING TO BE HEALED

We live in a society that has grown accustomed to instant gratification. Fast-food restaurants. Microwave popcorn. One-hour photo developing. TV news as it happens. Instantaneous Internet connections—ask a question, push a button, read your answer. At the dawning of the twenty-first century, nobody wants to wait for anything.

But sometimes the answer to our prayer is not seen instantaneously. A person's pathway to healing may require patience and persistence over an extended period of time.

I have personally witnessed several supernatural interventions when an individual was prayed for and *instantly, miraculously* was healed and made whole. I believe God can, and often does, step in to restore people to health in the twinkling of an eye. But in many instances, healing has been a process that occurred over weeks, months, and even longer periods of time.

In some cases I've seen patients who were doing well and whose condition was responding to a program of treatment. But after a short time, they got impatient or discouraged. They quit believing, stopped trying, discontinued praying, and gave up. Invariably their "quitter" attitude stopped or slowed the healing process.

The Bible preaches persistence and perseverance, and gives many examples of the necessity and value of a never-say-die attitude. One of the first is found in Genesis 32, which tells the story of Jacob wrestling with an angel all night long. Early in the morning, the angel said, "Let me go, for the day breaketh. And he said, I will not let thee go, except thou bless me" (v. 26 KJV).

This was a turning point in Jacob's life. Up to then he had been known as a deceiver and supplanter (which was actually the meaning of his name) for his shrewd dealings with his brother, his uncle, and others. But when he held on to the angel for a blessing, his name was changed to Israel, "for as a prince hast thou power with God and with men, and hast prevailed" (v. 28 KJV). Israel became the forefather of the Israelites, the children of God.

The Gospel of Luke relates two remarkable parables of Jesus' on the subject of importunity or persistence. The first comes in chapter 11, immediately after the Lord's Prayer. After teaching His disciples to pray and giving them a model, almost without taking a breath, Jesus told a story to illustrate the importance of persistence in praying.

A man went to his friend at midnight and said, "Lend me three loaves of bread. I have unexpected company and nothing in the house to eat." But his friend refused, saying that he'd already locked the door and put the children to bed. It was too much trouble to get up and rouse the whole household just to help him out.

Jesus suggested that the man ended up getting the bread he needed, not because of his neighbor's friendship, but because he wouldn't take no for an answer. "Though he will not rise and give him, because he is his friend, yet because of his importunity he will rise and give him as many as he needeth" (Luke 11:8 KJV).

This story is followed by one of the most-quoted and most-powerful verses in all of the Bible. Jesus said, "Ask, and it shall be given you; seek, and ye shall find; knock, and it shall be opened unto you" (Luke 11:9 KJV). I've heard that in the idiom of the original language, Jesus was really saying, "Ask, and keep on asking, seek, and keep on seeking, knock, and keep on knocking."

In the context of the entire passage, it seems certain that the Lord was instructing His disciples to pray and be persistent in prayer, never quitting or giving up.

Pray and Don't Faint

The second parable about persistent faith is found in Luke 18. The first verse of that chapter says, "And he spake a parable unto them to this end, that men ought always to pray, and not to faint" (KJV).

Known as the story of the unjust judge, Jesus told of a city where there was a judge who neither feared God nor regarded man. So when a woman came to him for justice, he ignored her at first. But she kept coming back and crying out. Eventually the judge said, "Even though I don't care anything about God or man, I'm going to see that this woman gets what she wants before she wears me out."

Jesus said, "Hear what the unjust judge said. Realize that God will respond to the pleas of His people and not keep putting them off" (see Luke 18:1–7).

Have you prayed to be healed and the answer has not come? Pray again and keep on praying. Don't give up. Be persistent. The Bible says, "Pray without ceasing" (1 Thess. 5:17 KJV).

Are you following a program of good health practices but the progress seems slow? Don't get discouraged. Remind yourself that the apostle Paul admonished, "And let us not be weary in well doing: for in due season we shall reap, if we faint not" (Gal. 6:9 KJV).

How often should you pray, and how long should you persevere? "Praying always with all prayer and supplication in the Spirit, and watching thereunto with all perseverance" (Eph. 6:18 KJV).

Be patient. Be faithful. Be determined. Keep praying and believing.

And hold on until the answer comes.

4. DEVELOP A "FEISTY" ATTITUDE

According to the dictionary, *feisty* means "spunky" or "having or showing a lively aggressiveness." It is just this attitude that a doctor likes to see in his patients, especially those facing real health challenges.

When disease or serious sickness has assaulted a person's body, all systems are marshaled to do battle. The brain sounds an alarm, calling every part of the body to help defend and repair the weak or injured part and to launch an all-out assault on any invading germs, viruses, allergens, or other enemies of the body.

The greatest danger at this point is that a patient will become passive, give up, or fail to resist and fight against the sickness or disease. A medical school dean once told a graduating class of new doctors, "Your skills will extend no further than a person's will to live. Any patient who has no will to live will defeat your best efforts."[1]

The Bible confirms the deadly danger of passivity. The Amplified version says, "He who does not use his endeavors to heal himself is brother to him who commits suicide" (Prov. 18:9).

A feisty patient awakens, stirs up, and undergirds his natural will to live through faith in God, trust in His Word, and ready cooperation with what he must do in the natural—his endeavors. He does not sit back and accept what is happening to his body, but focuses his attention and energy on the manifestation of healing.

The Bible says, "And from the days of John the Baptist until now the kingdom of heaven suffereth violence, and the violent take it by force" (Matt. 11:12 KJV). I believe this means that at times we must have a "lively aggressiveness" in claiming and taking possession of the promises that are ours as children of God. Also, we must have an attitude of violence and rise up against the darkness when we deal with the works of the devil and the principalities and powers of darkness spoken of in Ephesians 6:12.

How do we engage in this kind of spiritual warfare? By guarding our thoughts and our words. Paul said, "Casting down imaginations, and every high thing that exalteth itself against the knowledge of God, and bringing into captivity every thought to the obedience of Christ" (2 Cor. 10:5 KJV). Don't let your imagination run away with you. Don't give "high things" like medical tests and the opinions of specialists and bad reports more credence than the promises of God. Cut off every thought of defeat and hopelessness.

Realize the power of words. The Bible says, "Death and life are in the power of the tongue" (Prov. 18:21 KJV). Choose to speak life. If you are hurting and desperate for your body to win the battle over pain, disease, and destruction and you don't know what to say, speak God's Word. Say out loud, "The Word of God says that 'I shall not die, but live, and declare the works of the Lord. Bless the Lord, O my soul . . . who healeth all [my] diseases" (Ps. 118:17; 103:1, 3 KJV).

In my book *The Bible Cure*, I noted that when the kingdom of heaven was originally on this earth, there was no disease, sickness, illness, or affliction. "But now because of sin and our fallen nature, the devil has stolen what should be ours. We must violently take it back. So we declare by faith in the name and authority of Jesus Christ:

No, devil! In Jesus' name, I refuse to accept this disease in my body. In Jesus' name, I command this affliction to flee. My body is the temple of the Holy Spirit. I will not tolerate this attack of the enemy against my body. Disease has no right or authority to exist in my body, the temple of the Holy

Spirit, because I have been healed by the stripes, by the shed blood of Jesus Christ. In Jesus' name, I rebuke this sickness.[2]

5. FIND YOUR UNIQUE PATHWAY TO HEALING

In the early years of my medical practice as a Christian, I was puzzled by the different ways patients were healed. Although I prayed and depended on the power of the Holy Spirit to guide me, it seemed that no two patients received healing in exactly the same way. One might be healed supernaturally, solely through faith and the prayer of agreement. Another with almost identical symptoms would receive prayer but, in addition, natural or even prescription medicine, and then their healing would occur.

Then God showed me a biblical precedent or pattern, which was to become the guiding scriptural principle for my medical practice and subsequent ministry.

Matthew 9 tells of two blind men who came to Jesus to receive their sight. Jesus ministered to them just as I pictured in my mind that He should. He touched their eyes and their sight was immediately restored (see vv. 29–30).

Mark 8 also reports on the healing of a blind man. He was brought to Jesus, who spit on his eyes and put His hands on him. Then Jesus asked, "Do you see anything?" The man looked up and said he could see people, but they looked like trees walking around. So Jesus put His hands on the man's eyes again, and he could see clearly, his eyesight totally restored (see vv. 23–25).

John 9:6 speaks of Jesus' mixing clay and saliva and placing it on the eyes of still another blind man. After applying the mud, He told the man to go down a certain path, bend down into a pool, place water in his hands, and wash his eyes. As the man obeyed, he was healed. His sight was restored.

Now, suppose you could go to each of these blind men and ask, "What is the right way to be healed of blindness?" Two of them would say, "Well, Jesus just touches your eyes and instantly you can see."

Another would say, "It sounds strange, but Jesus spits on your eyes. Then He touches you a couple of times and your eyesight returns."

The last man would say, "First you have to have mud daubed on your eyes. Then you go to the pool of Siloam and wash it out. When you do, you can see!"

Do you get the point? In these three cases, Jesus dealt with the blind men in completely different ways. Only one thing was the same—they all were healed! At the end, each one could see.

Suddenly I saw what God was trying to show me. John 9:7 said the man "went his way"—he obeyed the Lord and came back seeing. The key principle is that *each person must follow a distinctive pathway to healing.* Just as the blind men were healed in different, individual ways, the manifestation of healing will come to each one of us in a unique way.

With God there is no universal, cookie-cutter, one-size-fits-all approach to healing. Just as no two people on earth have identical fingerprints, no two individuals will have exactly the same pathway to healing!

How does God heal? One person's pathway to healing may be a supernatural manifestation through the prayer of faith. Another's pathway leads to healing through God's anointing on a natural substance—something we can touch, see, hold, and experience through our senses. God may use traditional medicine, a mineral, a plant, an herb. He may use something as commonplace as the vitamins and chemicals in certain foods, or something as dramatic as a surgical procedure. But the bottom line is that when each individual finds his pathway to healing and follows it, God will lead him each step of the way to healing.

Expect God's Best

How will you find your *pathway to healing?* For me, the key is praying and being open to the revelation and leading of the Holy Spirit. I always encourage my patients to receive whatever method the Lord impresses us to follow. Don't be limited by preconceived notions or expectations. If we just let God move as He chooses, giving complete liberty to the Holy Spirit, His best for us will happen in our lives, and we will receive our healings.

Do you remember the Bible story of Naaman the leper? This influential, powerful man sought out Elisha, the prophet, hoping to be healed of his disease. He assumed that the prophet would come out to meet him, pray to the Lord, and cure him instantly. That's the way he thought it should be done.

Instead, Elisha didn't even quit what he was doing. He sent a servant with a message for Naaman that said, "Go wash yourself seven times in the Jordan and your flesh will be cleansed and restored" (see 2 Kings 5:10).

Naaman got very upset. No doubt his ego was hurt that Elisha didn't even come to meet him. His pride was hurt at the thought of dipping himself in the muddy waters of the Jordan instead of some cleaner, nicer river. And he was shocked at being asked to do something totally different from what he thought was the right way to get healed. So he went off in a rage, mad at Elisha and mad at God.

But he was still a leper. He still desperately needed to be healed.

Someone finally talked some sense into Naaman, and he decided to follow God's pathway to healing for him. That meant setting aside his expectations and surrendering to God's way. That meant going down to the Jordan and dipping seven times in its muddy waters.

It also meant he got healed. When he came up out of the water on that seventh dip, the leprosy was gone. Naaman looked down at his hands, arms, legs, and feet. They were unblemished, smooth, and whole. They had been washed clean in the muddy waters!

You may be feeling as Naaman felt. You may be angry with God and with other servants of the Lord—Christian doctors and pastors—because they have not responded in the way you expected. Do you want to hear from God and be healed, or do you want to keep going around the mountain of your illness?[3]

God has a pathway of healing for you. It is His plan and His will for you. If you want to find it, He will reveal it to you. You will find it when you find Him. God says, "Ye shall seek me, and find me, when ye shall search for me with all your heart" (Jer. 29:13 KJV).

6. GOD USES THE NATURAL AND THE SUPERNATURAL TO HEAL

All healing comes from God. The Bible says He is the Source of all good things and never changes. "Every good gift and every perfect gift is from above, and cometh down from the Father of lights, with whom is no variableness, neither shadow of turning" (James 1:17 KJV).

Whatever pathway we follow to our healing, or whatever means is employed to bring it to us, the healing is the same. Supernatural healing is not necessarily better than healing that also involves the natural because in both cases, God is the Healer.

Very few doctors I have ever known claimed to heal people in their own wisdom and power. They could perform various therapies, prescribe certain medications, explain the scientific laws of cause and effect relative to the problem, and give advice on how to take care of the affected area of the body. Then all they could do was step back and wait for the healing power God has placed in the human body to go to work.

As we've already discussed, God's original healing plan was for man not to get sick in the first place. And to help make this possible, He carefully, meticulously taught man which foods to eat and which to avoid. Four thousand years later, science is still discovering that some of the foods God put on the approved list actually have chemical properties that prevent and destroy disease, while foods on the "don't eat" list actually can cause or contribute to deadly killers like heart disease and cancer.

The Word of God tells us that no curse is causeless. "As the bird by wandering, as the swallow by flying, so the curse causeless shall not come" (Prov. 26:2 KJV). Another translation says, "An undeserved curse does not come to rest" (NIV). Sickness and disease are curses, but often there is a cause or a reason for them to attack. Failure to observe God's laws about natural things like food can make our bodies more susceptible to destructive attacks.

We also know that God's anointing can rest on natural substances. Nearly half of all prescription drugs come from substances found in plants. And scientific research is confirming the healing qualities or healthful effects of many herbs, minerals, vitamins, and nutritional supplements.

I believe with all my heart that following God's guidelines for a healthy lifestyle—proper diet, stress management, and a proper balance of work and rest—will lessen our bodies' risk of contracting sickness and disease. I also believe that, as a general rule, God asks us to do what we can do in the natural as He acts in our behalf in the supernatural.

Some people trust only in certain methods of healing. That's not the best way. There are too many surgeries being performed. There is too much medication being prescribed. There are pathways that God has for His people that deviate from standard, traditional medicine and treatment as taught in medical school.

On the other hand, there are Christians who believe only in supernatural methods of healing. If they are not healed by laying on of hands and prayer, through a miraculous intervention, then they will not be healed at all.

The truth is, in my opinion, that it is the height of presumption for anyone to dictate to God the pathway to His healing! The proper attitude is to pray with an open mind, seeking God's pathway. "The steps of a good man are ordered by the LORD: and he delighteth in his way" (Ps. 37:23 KJV). The Lord may use either supernatural or natural means, or a combination of both. God uses doctors, medicines, herbs, nutrition, supplements, exercise, prayer, and miraculous interventions of all kinds to heal us. But He wants to heal us, and He will.

Let your voice cry out to God today in the words of Jeremiah: "Heal me, O LORD, and I shall be healed; save me, and I shall be saved" (17:14 KJV).

7

God Still Heals Today:

CASE HISTORIES OF PATIENTS WHO FOUND THEIR PATHWAY TO HEALING THROUGH PRAYER

During my years of clinical medical practice specializing in diagnostic and preventive medicine, I have examined and treated literally thousands of patients. In addition to the executives and corporate employees from the Houston area who came to me each year for complete, detailed physical exams, hundreds of other individuals from all over the United States came seeking help for a bewildering array of maladies, sicknesses, and diseases.

Very often patients told us that we were their last hope, that they had been to many doctors, clinics, and hospitals, and had found no help. Either their specific cases had not been diagnosed, or the physicians they had consulted felt there was no cure or therapy that would be effective in controlling or improving their condition.

In my practice, I have always given my patients a thorough head-to-toe physical examination, a battery of body chemistry tests, an exhaustive medical history, and any specialized tests such as X rays, EKGs, treadmill stress tests, or other diagnostic procedures that seem appropriate for the symptoms.

Once I had the test findings, medical history, and any other patient information before me, I invariably found myself praying for inspiration, insight, wisdom, and guidance.

I asked the Holy Spirit to reveal to me the root of the patient's problem and to enable me to help the sufferer discover his or her own personal pathway to healing.

I do not consider myself smarter or better than a host of other able, dedicated doctors. But I have often been blessed to sense the personal presence of God near me as I searched for ways to bring healing to people. I believe God is a healing God and that His heart and Spirit are sensitive and supportive to those who labor to destroy sickness and disease and to alleviate pain.

Time after time, as I breathed a prayer, I would see a recognizable pattern in the data before me and immediately know the problem and the treatment. Sometimes I would remember a lecture from medical school, an article from a medical journal, or some other case I'd had in the past that provided the key to treating my current patient.

At times I'd feel that conventional medical treatment was indicated, or perhaps a medical protocol of prescription drugs plus the use of certain herbs, minerals, food supplements, and other natural substances—a complementary treatment program.

And I always included prayer. On numerous occasions I felt that nothing medically should be done, that all that was necessary was the prayer of faith. What a glorious experience to pray for a suffering individual and to see the frown of pain fade away and a glow of joy and thanksgiving light up his face. Sometimes this happened miraculously and instantaneously. At other times gradual improvement occurred over a period of a few days or weeks.

But even if I prescribed medicines or other natural treatments, I would also prescribe prayer—specific, directed prayer. Prayer filled with faith, trust, and thanksgiving to God. Positive, believing, motivating prayer.

This balanced approach, a combining of the natural and the supernatural, has been wonderfully effective. I have received literally hundreds and hundreds of follow-up reports from patients—testimonies to God's healing power. I want to share several of these case histories with you later in this chapter.

First, though, let's review some of the important information covered in previous chapters. I encourage you to go back and study the six biblical foundations for healing in detail. It may even be helpful to highlight or underline the key words or phrases that stand out to you. We've recapped them here for you:

1. Have faith—actively believe—that God wants you to be healed and whole.

2. Realize the price that God has already paid for your healing through Jesus' sacrifice.

3. Be persistent in seeking your healing.

4. Have a "feisty" attitude—a never-give-up fighting spirit to possess what God has for you.

5. Seek to discover and then follow your own personal pathway to healing. Keep in mind the blind man in John 9:7—as he went his way, he was healed. This is the foundational Scripture for praying specifically for your unique pathway to healing.

6. Recognize the role of both the natural and the supernatural in your journey to recovery. Healing anointing can flow through natural substances, or happen miraculously and instantaneously through spiritual intervention, or occur

through a combination of natural substances and the supernatural.

Another truth I want to reemphasize is that you must be willing to do all you can do to be healed. Proverbs 18:9 in the Amplified Bible says, "He who does not use his endeavors to heal himself is brother to him who commits suicide." Are you being diligent in the things you know you should—or should not—be doing? Are you following a proper diet, getting adequate exercise, resting enough, avoiding stress overloads, following the pathway to healing God has for you? If you don't do these things, how long will it take for your body to break down again even if you are healed of your current affliction?

Take some positive action. Only as we do all we can do to be healthy can we reasonably expect God to do what we can't do! I encourage you to pray and ask God, "Are there certain endeavors or actions I must take in the natural to see my healing manifested? Show me. Help me."

Last, believe, accept, and *practice* the words of Jesus in Mark 11:23—"whosoever shall say unto this mountain, Be thou removed, and be thou cast into the sea; and shall not doubt in his heart, but shall believe that those things which he saith shall come to pass; he shall have whatsoever he saith" (KJV). Notice that Jesus didn't say to pray in general for God's will to be done, or even to say, "Lord, I'm troubled because this mountain is in my way. Please do something to help me." Do you see that?

The Lord said, "Speak to your mountain." Command it to be removed. Command it to leave you—"be thou cast into the sea." Then He says if we don't doubt, but believe that our specific declarations will come to pass, we will have what we say.

This is an awesome, powerful promise. Can you understand the unlimited capability God has placed in our control?

Now use this power in prayer by finding out specifically what is wrong and out of order in your body. Have your doctor explain it to you in detail. Write it down if you need to. Once you have this information in hand, you are ready to apply Mark 11:23 to your personal situation. Your specific physical problem is the mountain you have to speak to and command to be cast into the sea in order to have your health restored.

CASE HISTORIES

Now let's see how these principles were applied in some real-life cases from my own medical practice. Names have been changed and certain circumstances may have been deleted to protect the privacy of individuals, but each case history does represent a real person who faced a major health problem.

Case One

Frank Wilson traveled from the East Coast to consult with me about a debilitating problem that had been going on for more than ten years. His problem was extremely embarrassing to him because it affected his intestinal tract. He was having up to fifteen bowel movements daily with accompanying mucus and blood. The cramping, pain, and frequency of bowel movements kept him from doing his work as a minister. He had sought prayer from some of the most prominent preachers and healing evangelists, but to no avail. He had been to multiple medical specialists and had been on large doses of medications but, again, found no relief. He had done everything he knew to do to deal with this problem, but nothing seemed to work.

Finally Frank came to Houston and began describing this desperate story to me. I examined him, and after gathering information about his body through various tests, I had him come into my office and began to explain to him the nature of the problem. He had a disease known as ulcerative colitis, which is an inflammatory disease affecting the intestinal area. Led by the Holy Spirit, I began describing to him the mountain that he was facing. I told him the exact cause of this disease was not known to medical science, but it was thought to be the result of a misdirected immune system attacking the lining of the intestine. Various cells of the immune system, such as lymphocytes and other components, were literally attacking his own body, resulting in the inflammation and bleeding.

As I spoke, I could see the expression on Frank's face begin to change from desperation to hope. No explanation had ever been given to him about the cause of his problem, and therefore he did not understand the mountain he had to speak to. He was eager to combat the assault on his body but felt frustrated because of his lack of awareness as to the specific schemes and devices the enemy was using to attack him. As I gave Frank an abbreviated medical description of what was causing his problem, I explained how he was to pray and speak to his body: he was to speak to his immune system and command it to become balanced rather than overreactive. Then, when the immune system became balanced, the inflammation in the lining of his intestine would dissipate and the distressing symptoms he was experiencing would cease.

As we prayed together, I agreed with him in prayer for his immune system imbalance to be resolved. In addition, we asked God to reveal Frank's unique pathway to healing. I felt that the Lord showed me to have Frank use certain vitamin and mineral supplements that would help to balance his immune system (such as selenium, vitamin E, and glutathione). I also felt directed to prescribe fish oil capsules, which contain omega 3 fatty acids (EPA and DHA). Studies have shown that this particular fatty acid can decrease inflammation in the colon.

After I prayed with Frank and outlined the various natural things he was to do, he felt an increased sense of hope and faith for his healing. He later told me what happened to him after he left the clinic that day.

On the trip home he had some of the worst abdominal cramping and pain he had ever experienced. The powers of darkness were stirred up against him, and he had every opportunity to be discouraged and tell himself that "nothing really happened to you in Houston." He resisted these negative thoughts because he knew in his spirit that he had found his pathway to healing. Though the pain and bowel abnormalities lasted for several hours, he continued to thank God that the manifestation of healing was on the way, and he continued speaking specifically to the "mountain" as we had outlined earlier.

Frank told me that he woke up the next day and there were no symptoms in his body. The pain was gone. The cramping was gone. From that day on, his bowel movements were normal. A year later, he still had a good report. He is once again able to fulfill God's call on his life, set free from the destructive forces of darkness that he had experienced for years. May the glory go to God for this dramatic healing.

Case Two

Gloria Atkinson, a lady in her sixties, came to see me complaining of heart palpitations. She felt her heart beating irregularly with occasional rapid bursts of activity. She had no other symptoms associated with this, but she felt that God was directing her to get a further evaluation of this condition. After checking her, I determined that she had what is known as atrial fibrillation. This is a rhythm disturbance affecting the upper chambers of the heart. The small chambers at the top of the heart beat with an irregular rhythm independently of the rest of the heart. This quivering motion of the heart muscle is a potentially serious cause of stroke. As the muscle beats irregularly, the blood flow in the chamber is disrupted and the blood can form a clot. This clot then migrates to the lower ventricle, or pumping chamber of the heart, and can be expelled from the heart directly into the brain, leading to a stroke. Fortunately, this woman had no sign of blood clots or a stroke, but I knew that either the heart would have to be restored back to a normal rhythm or Gloria would have to be on blood thinners the rest of her life.

I explained to her in detail what was happening in her heart, and this became a focal point of her prayers. She could now speak specifically to the muscle in the upper chamber of her heart and, in Jesus' name, she could command the rhythm to become regular. In addition, she could bind the formation of a blood clot, which could break loose and produce a stroke. God's hand of protection had been upon her, but He was now warning Gloria of the potential danger and giving us a specific way to pray. As we sought God together for her complete pathway to healing, I was led to recommend that she consult with a cardiologist I had worked with for many years.

Gloria went to the cardiologist, and he confirmed that she did have atrial fibrillation and, apparently, had had it a long time. In the natural, atrial fibrillation is a very difficult problem to solve when it has been present for a prolonged period. The cardiologist told Gloria the only possible way to correct her condition would be to initiate an electrical shock to her heart. She really did not want to do this (who would?), but she consented to return to him for the procedure. Prior to her return visit, she earnestly prayed, speaking daily to the "mountain" and believing God for a complete manifestation of healing.

Upon her return to the doctor two weeks later, instead of Gloria getting shocked, the cardiologist was shocked! Gloria's atrial fibrillation had completely converted to a normal rhythm (sinus rhythm). She did not need any blood-thinning medication. The palpitations had ceased, and she was placed on a one-pill-daily medication to keep her heart in normal rhythm. In his follow-up letter to me, the cardiologist expressed his surprise and amazement at the sudden turn of events as Gloria's heart became normal. She had found her pathway to healing without the use of major shock therapy, and she was spared the potential effects of a disabling stroke. She did all that she knew to do in the natural, and God did the supernatural!

Case Three

Jonathan Collins, a distinguished businessman, came to the clinic for a medical evaluation, and during the course of his exam I noted a nodule on his prostate gland. His PSA blood level (a test for prostate cancer) was normal, but the PSA level is normal in a small percentage of men who, in fact, do have prostate cancer. This nodule was particularly ominous as prostate cancer is the most common malignancy in older men and is particularly prominent in men of Afro-American descent.

As Jonathan and I prayed about his pathway to healing concerning this nodule, the Spirit of God led us in a direction contrary to conventional medical treatment. Though the traditional approach is to do an ultrasound-guided biopsy of nodules this size, we felt directed to do nothing in this situation except pray. I prayed the prayer of agreement with Jonathan, speaking directly to this nodule according to Mark 11:23, commanding it to shrink and disappear. I further spoke to his immune system to become activated and attack any abnormal cells that might be present in his prostate. I felt the Lord gave us another specific directive—that Jonathan was to return to the clinic in three months for a repeat evaluation and examination of the prostate.

When he returned three months later, the nodule, the location of which I carefully noted in the right lobe of his prostate, was totally gone! His prostate gland was normal.

Our God is not a god of foolishness. When a supernatural healing occurs, it can be documented and will stand up to medical scrutiny. While we do not have to have scientific evidence that God is a healer, documenting medical healing such as this gives glory to God, and confirmed testimonies like this give hope to others and stir faith in God as our

Healer. Medical experts might say, "Well, this was just a spontaneous remission, or just an area of inflammation." I say that a spontaneous remission such as this, which at last check had lasted for more than two years, is a *healing*!

Case Four

Marilyn Nelson, a Christian lady, came to me with various troubling symptoms. The minute I saw her, I knew she sensed that something serious was attacking her body. She had read our books and watched us on our television program, *The Doctor and the Word,* and she wanted to know how to pray for her condition. She also wanted to find what she could do in the natural.

Marilyn had developed a peculiar skin rash and went to a rheumatologist. The blood test he ran indicated an elevated sed rate (ESR). The rheumatologist said she was possibly developing lupus, an autoimmune disease, but that it was "too soon to tell." With a feisty attitude, she determined that she was not going to sit back and wait for something to develop. She sensed in her spirit that she needed to take action quickly.

As I took Marilyn's medical history, I sensed her strong faith. I said, "You really didn't come to see me. You came to have me help you to seek God's pathway for your health." Tears began running down her cheeks as she nodded assent. As I examined her, I found no signs of lupus, although she did have certain skin and joint changes. These factors, coupled with the mild elevation in her sed rate, convinced me that she would eventually develop full-blown lupus in her body if we did not act.

After the exam, I explained to Marilyn the nature of lupus

and what we needed to speak to and stand against. I explained how lupus is a disease in which the body literally turns against itself. The body's own immune system begins attacking various organs such as the kidneys, the joints, the skin, the heart, and other areas. I painted a picture for her of the various T-cells, B-cells, and other components of the immune system. We then formulated this information into a prayer as we spoke to her mountain.

In the name of Jesus, we commanded that her immune system become balanced and that the components of the immune system would reset themselves and not recognize normal body organs as being foreign invaders. God designed the immune system to rise up and attack invaders such as bacteria, viruses, and even abnormally developing cells that become cancerous. But with lupus, the immune system literally turns against its own body.

Marilyn understood the specific way to pray daily to block the development of lupus and to pray her immune system into balance. In addition, God's pathway also involved using natural components from the plant kingdom in the form of supplements that would help balance the immune system. We placed her on various antioxidants (vitamins C, E, and selenium), as well as certain amino acids such as glutathione, which have been shown to have a positive effect on the immune system.

Several years have elapsed since I first saw this patient. Marilyn's skin rash has disappeared and she has no symptoms of lupus in her body at all. Again, prayers were answered.

Case Five

I had the privilege of seeing Harold Williams, a precious gentleman who had been a missionary. While serving on the mission field, he had been imprisoned and severely wounded during an attack by other prisoners. As a result of the stab wounds he sustained, he had contracted hepatitis C. This is a viral infection that attacks the liver and can lead to chronic hepatitis, cirrhosis of the liver, and liver cancer.

Prior to seeing me, Harold had undergone a liver biopsy, which had revealed the presence of scar tissue in his liver. His liver enzymes were elevated, indicating continued inflammation in his liver caused by the activity of a virus. After our evaluation, we determined that there was, in fact, hepatitis C virus in his body. Traditional medicine offers a drug called interferon, but it has proved to be a benefit in only a minority of cases. Harold wanted to pursue natural remedies to prevent liver disease from progressing.

I shared with him how his lymphocytes and other immune system cells were designed by God to overcome viruses and other foreign invaders. In his case, we needed the immune system to be activated and to recognize, seek out, and destroy the virus in his body. This became the specific mountain that he was to take authority over according to Mark 11:23. This became a daily prayer for him. In addition, I felt God directing us to an herb known as milk thistle, which can help regenerate liver cells and strengthen liver function. So I placed him on a prescription of directed prayer, vitamin supplements, and milk thistle. Harold returned to the clinic for a follow-up several weeks later, and his liver enzyme count had dropped dramatically. His liver was being rejuvenated as an activated immune system overcame the virus attacking this vital organ.

After several years, Harold's liver tests became normal and stayed in the normal range. He will never face the destruction of his liver and potential for cirrhosis, cancer, or a liver transplant. How can I say this with such assurance? Because God gave us a specific plan to follow, both in the supernatural realm of prayer and in the natural realm of herbal plant substances. I know Harold is healed. He knows he is healed. And that settles it. This is the true essence of faith.

Case Six

Charles Cunningham walked into my office with an obvious look of worry on his face. As I began reviewing his history, I noted that this older gentleman had indeed been through a lot. Two or three years before I saw him, he had developed chest and shoulder pain. Additional testing ultimately revealed blockages in his arteries. He had undergone an angioplasty procedure (balloon dilation) due to blockage in the coronary arteries that carry blood to the heart. The procedure had been successful, and the symptoms in his body had disappeared.

Prior to his heart problem, Charles had prostate cancer and had undergone surgery to remove his prostate gland (radical prostatectomy). This, too, had been successful.

The reason for his current visit was that he had once again developed chest and shoulder pain. Charles was concerned to the point of worry and anxiety. As I spoke with him and examined him, I was praying for guidance, wisdom, and direction. I began to get the distinct impression in my spirit that there was nothing physically wrong with him. I confirmed this by doing a thorough evaluation. Could the chest and shoulder pain be due to additional artery blockage?

Could he have metastatic prostate cancer that had spread to his bones? I didn't think so, but he needed a confirmation.

I did a stress test, and Charles's heart checked out perfectly, with normal blood flow through all of the major arteries. He had no chest pain or symptoms during the course of the test. His digital exam where the prostate used to be showed nothing out of the ordinary, and his blood PSA levels were almost undetectable, which was what we wanted to see.

I went into my office and prayed, literally asking God, "What is wrong with this man?" The answer was immediate—"He is filled with fear and worry." I was convinced that fear was his whole problem. None of the medical tests contradicted this diagnosis. I then talked to this man and told him the good news that his heart tests were normal, his prostate follow-up tests were normal, and all of the other body system checks were normal. Why did I begin this way? Because the Bible says good news is health to the bones (see Prov. 16:24). If anyone needed good news, he did.

Charles then asked the obvious question, "What about my chest and shoulder pain?"

"The symptoms in your body are due to fear and worry," I said. "Your body has been through a lot, and you should not feel condemned because fear has attacked you. We must get you released from this fear, and with God's help, we will."

Tears welled up in Charles's eyes. He was a strong, muscular man, but he was almost sobbing as he said, "Yes, I am afraid. I have a wife who needs me, and she has already been through so much with my health."

I reassured him that he was going to be fine. I then showed him 1 Peter 5:7 in the Amplified Bible, which says, "Casting the whole of your care [all your anxieties, all your worries, all your concerns, once and for all] on Him, for He cares for you affectionately and cares about you watchfully." I directed him to read this Scripture himself and to put it into practice by casting his fear and worry about possible diseases onto God. We prayed together, and I literally could feel the comforting power of the Holy Spirit flow out of me and into his body. He, too, sensed the peace that passeth understanding. When we finished praying, we both had to wipe away tears. Charles had been set free.

The chest and shoulder pain never returned, and to this day he remains free of any heart problems or any evidence of prostate cancer. God gave us no specific things to do in the natural. Fear can be just as destructive as any heart or cancer problem, and once the Holy Spirit illuminated the problem, the solution was all in the supernatural realm involving faith, prayer, and acting on the Word of God.

Case Seven

A young woman named Amy Russell scheduled an appointment, and when I saw her, the first words out of her mouth were, "I have been to eight specialists for my symptoms. I'm not getting better; I'm getting worse."

I thought, *Where have I heard this before?* I knew it was in Mark 5, which describes a woman with an issue of blood who had suffered at the hands of many physicians and spent all the money she had.

Amy reviewed her medical history with me, and she had been given nearly every test in the book. Her blood work was normal. MRI imaging tests were normal. Nerve conduction studies were normal—in fact, all of her extensive tests were normal. I conducted my own tests and everything I checked was normal.

Something was obviously wrong, however. She was having numbness and loss of feeling in both her upper and lower extremities. Though her hormone levels were normal, she would suddenly break out in sweats. She had heart palpitations, irregular beats, and at times she experienced shortness of breath and difficulty catching her breath. She had lost her appetite and was finding it difficult to sleep well at night. She had to push herself to accomplish simple things around her house. She was losing interest in her career and in her former interests, such as playing the piano. She noticed that her thinking was cloudy, as she was having difficulty making up her mind about even simple things. Amy had periods of both anxiety as well as sadness that she attributed to the multiple symptoms in her body. This was a case to take before the throne of God.

After finishing her exam, I departed to my office and closed the door. I began praying, "God, this is a tough one. I need Your help and revelation knowledge to uncover the works of darkness that have attacked this woman. She has suffered long enough, and I want to help set her free." The Spirit of God suddenly impressed on my spirit, *She has a serotonin/neurotransmitter chemical imbalance.* I lifted my head from prayer and said, "Thank You, Lord. Of course, that's it. All of her symptoms now make sense."

There is no blood test or any other test that can specifically identify the imbalance of various chemicals in the brain, such as serotonin, norepinephrine, and dopamine. These chemicals allow the brain to communicate within itself and with the rest of the body. They are collectively known as neurotransmitters since they transmit impulses between nerve endings. When these chemicals get out of balance (usually depleted), the brain literally misinterprets the signals it receives. It thinks the arms and legs are numb when, in reality, the sensory nerves in this area are normal. The chemicals control the appetite centers of the brain, the sleep centers of the brain, and the centers that regulate breathing. This explained Amy's shortness of breath. The imbalance in the chemicals can also cause feelings of anxiety, triggering chemical releases that lead to heart irregularities as well as sweats.

Now that I had a diagnosis, we needed a pathway that would lead to the manifestation of healing and the resolution of Amy's symptoms. I explained to her about the neurotransmitters and what happens when they get out of balance. As she understood the specific mountain she was facing, I told her how to pray, speaking to the serotonin and other chemicals that were out of balance and commanding them to be normal and to conduct nerve transmission according to God's design. I instructed her to rebuke the spirit of fear if the symptoms came and to speak to her body, commanding it to line up with God's Word. The various symptoms she was having were very real but were not due to any damage to her nerves or other organs. God had revealed the root cause of the problem, and she could now pray specifically.

In addition, God instructed us to use a prescription medication that would help bring the chemicals into balance on the natural side. She was reluctant at first, saying, "I don't want to be on medicines all my life."

"Forget that," I said. "You will be on one pill a day for three to four months and then you will taper off of it. This was God's instruction to me." Knowing that God had intervened on her behalf, Amy agreed to follow His instruction.

Within days, her symptoms began subsiding. She began playing the piano again, and she was literally a different person—her old self. In four months we gradually took her off the medication, and she has had no further symptoms at all. This healing could be right out of the ninth chapter of John. John 9:7 tells about a blind man who was healed as he went his way. So, too, as Amy "went her way," she was healed. She had faith in God as her Healer and followed a set of instructions that He gave, which involved a natural substance. She was obedient, and the time came when the natural substance was removed. Then, just like the blind man in John 9, she was totally healed.

Some say that the day of miracles and supernatural healings is over. There never was a *day* of miracles and healing, only a *God* of miracles and healing. He is an unchangeable God who still heals and sets people free from the curse of disease. I pray that these case histories will give you renewed hope and faith in the great and mighty God who sent His only Son to bear our diseases and infirmities, as well as our sins, and to set men free.

8

THE MOST IMPORTANT
PRAYER YOU'LL EVER PRAY

The most important thing you can do for your health and well-being is to find forgiveness for your sins by accepting Jesus Christ as your personal Savior and being born again into the family of God.

Sin? Do I, a modern man of science, really believe in the concepts of right and wrong and personal responsibility, in the idea of old-fashioned sin? *Absolutely.* I personally have felt the inner turmoil and sense of alienation that told me I was not right with God. I also have experienced the unspeakable joy of being cleansed of unrighteousness and restored to fellowship with my Creator and established in a vital, personal relationship with God as my Father.

As a physician, I have treated hundreds of patients with various illnesses and afflictions that I believe were brought on or made worse by the "disease" and unwell condition of their inner being. How could anyone expect to live wrong and continue in health for long?

The greatest healing you can receive is in your spirit. The psalmist David cried, "O LORD, have mercy on me; heal me, for I have sinned against you" (Ps. 41:4 NIV).

If you're already a believer, you understand the benefits of living without guilt and being energized daily by the power of perfect love. The Bible says that a life controlled by God, a life filled with the Holy Spirit, will be wonderfully new. "But when the Holy Spirit controls our lives he will produce this kind of fruit in us: love, joy, peace, patience, kindness, goodness, faithfulness, gentleness and self-control" (Gal. 5:22–23 TLB).

If you haven't yet come to God for salvation, I have good news for you! God loves you and has a wonderful plan for your life. It makes no difference whether you have tried to live a good moral life but failed, or if you have plunged to the depths of degradation. Jesus paid the price for your sin through His death on the cross. His grace is sufficient for you.

Paul the Apostle was one of the greatest men who ever lived. Before he became a follower of Jesus, he tried to earn his way to God through religion. He spent his whole life studying the Jewish laws, and aggressively worked his way to the highest level of the strict sect of the Pharisees. But he did not find peace.

Even after he became a Christian, at first he struggled to attain perfection in his own strength and ability—to no avail. Listen to the anguish of his heart:

I don't understand myself at all, for I really want to do what is right, but I can't. I do what I don't want to—what I hate. I know perfectly well that what I am doing is wrong, and my bad conscience proves that I agree with these laws I am breaking. But I can't help myself, because I'm no longer doing it. It is sin inside me that is stronger than I am that makes me do these evil things.

I know I am rotten through and through so far as my old sinful nature is concerned. No matter which way I turn I can't make myself do right. I want to but I can't. When I want to do good, I don't; and when I try not to do wrong, I do it any-way. Now if I am doing what I don't want to, it is plain where the trouble is: sin still has me in its evil grasp . . .

So you see how it is: my new life tells me to do right, but the old nature that is still inside me loves to sin. Oh, what a terrible predicament I'm in! (Rom. 7:15–20, 24 TLB)

Have you ever felt that way—that it was hopeless for you to try to change your ways? Then pay attention to what comes next. Paul went on to say, "Who will free me from my slavery to this deadly lower nature? Thank God! It has been done by Jesus Christ our Lord. He has set me free" (Rom. 7:24–25 TLB).

Paul said that Jesus Christ made him into a new person. Jesus set him free from the attitudes and bondage of his old life. And I'm here to tell you that He will do the same for you.

WHAT YOU NEED TO KNOW TO BECOME A CHRISTIAN

There are four basic Scripture passages that outline what you need to know to become a part of the family of God. They are not complicated or hard to understand. Let them be your stepping-stones to a new life.

First, the Bible says, "All have sinned and fall short of the glory of God" (Rom. 3:23 NIV). Sinfulness is universal, a fun-damental part of the human condition. "All" doesn't leave anybody out. So we must start by knowing where we stand in God's eyes.

Second, there is a penalty for sin. The Bible says, "The wages of sin is death" (Rom. 6:23 NIV). That's pretty drastic, isn't it? Sin is no laughing matter. No wonder it casts such a dark shadow on our pathway and hangs such a heavy load on our shoulders. We are sinners, and the penalty for sin is death. Is there any hope for us? Is there any way of escape?

Third, yes. Someone else has already paid the penalty for our sin! The Bible says, "While we were still sinners, Christ died for us" (Rom. 5:8 NIV). Isn't that amazing? Why should He love us so? What a tremendous sacrifice Jesus made on our behalf. What a wonderful gift is ours!

Fourth, we can claim the benefit of Christ's sacrifice only as we confess that our lives belong to Him—that He is Lord. We must also believe that He is alive, resurrected from the death He died on the cross for us. As we do these two things, we are saved. The Bible says, "That if you confess with your mouth, 'Jesus is Lord,' and believe in your heart that God raised him from the dead, you will be saved. For it is with your heart that you believe and are justified, and it is with your mouth that you confess and are saved" (Rom. 10:9–10 NIV). Also, "If we confess our sins, he is faithful and just and will forgive us our sins and purify us from all unrighteousness" (1 John 1:9 NIV).

That's it—that's all you need to know and do to become a born-again Christian.

Born again? Yes, Jesus Himself used that term to describe the new life He gives to those who come to Him. He told a Pharisee named Nicodemus that no one could see the kingdom of God unless he was born again—"born of water and the Spirit. Flesh gives birth to flesh, but the Spirit gives birth to spirit" (John 3:5–6 NIV).

When you are born again, you relate to God in a new

way. He is not simply your Creator but your Father, and you are His child. "Yet to all who received him, to those who believed in his name, he gave the right to become children of God—children born not of natural descent, nor of human decision or a husband's will, but born of God" (John 1:12–13 NIV). This is a new and very special relationship.

The Bible also says, "Therefore if any man be in Christ, he is a new creature: old things are passed away; behold, all things are become new" (2 Cor. 5:17 KJV).

Are you ready for a new life? Pray this prayer with me:

Father in heaven, have mercy upon me, a sinner. I recognize that I have failed to please You with my life and way of living, and that my sins have separated me from You. I am sorry for my sins and ask Your forgiveness. Wash me and cleanse me because of the sacrifice of Your Son, Jesus. Lord Jesus, I accept You as my Savior and invite You to live in my heart and life. Send Your Holy Spirit to teach me and guide me step-by-step according to the plan You have for my life. I give myself to You. Help me to live for You and to do Your will in all that I say and do from this day forward. I love You and thank You for saving me—from my sin and for Your glory. Amen.

If you prayed and meant it, God has heard and answered your prayer. You are forgiven. Old things are passed away and all things have become new. You are a new creation, born again into new life in Christ. Welcome to the family of God!

Now, as a new Christian, you need to grow and become strong in your faith. The step you have taken is not the end but a glorious new beginning. The best way to find the daily nurture and care you need is by talking to God in prayer. Don't worry about *thee's* and *thou's* and theology. Just talk to God like a Father. Talk to Him daily, hourly, without ceasing. You are never alone.

Then begin learning about God and His will for you through reading His Word, the Holy Bible. Yes, you can understand it. The more you read it, the more meaningful it will become. I'd suggest starting with the Gospel of John in a modern translation that's easy to understand. You'll also be blessed by the Psalms and Proverbs. Don't try to read the whole Bible all at once, just read some every day. Open your mind and let the Lord speak to you through the Scriptures.

It's very important for you to make some Christian friends and start associating with other believers who can encourage and assist you in your walk with God. Find a good church that offers both support and opportunity for Christian service and teaches you the Word of God.

Don't try to go too fast or get impatient with your progress. God will make Himself real to you and help you. Remember, you've been born again and are a spiritual infant. You need time to grow in strength, knowledge, and wisdom.

I'd be so happy to hear from you and to know of your decision for Christ. Please write to me, Reginald B. Cherry, M.D., P.O. Box 27711, Houston, Texas 77227.

THE HEALING WORD

"HE SENT FORTH HIS WORD AND
HEALED THEM." (PS. 107:20 NIV)

The Holy Bible is the Word of God. Within its pages are revealed God's perfect will and plan for mankind, the answers to life's hardest questions, and instructions on how to be healed and to live in wholeness and health.

I believe the following scriptural passages are healing words from God for anyone suffering from sickness or disease. If you are seeking healing for your body, I encourage you to read these verses aloud daily. They will build and strengthen your faith and form a solid spiritual foundation for your recovery.

If you listen carefully to the voice of the LORD your God and do what is right in his eyes, if you pay attention to his commands and keep all his decrees, I will not bring on you any of the diseases I brought on the Egyptians, for I am the LORD, who heals you. (Ex. 15:26 NIV)

Worship the LORD your God, and his blessing will be on your food and water. I will take away sickness from among you . . . I will give you a full life span. (Ex. 23:25–26 NIV)

The LORD will keep you free from every disease. (Deut. 7:15 NIV)

I have set before you life and death, blessings and curses. Now choose life, so that you and your children may live and that you may love the LORD your God, listen to his voice, and hold fast to him. For the LORD is your life, and he will give you many years in the land he swore to give to your fathers, Abraham, Isaac and Jacob. (Deut. 30:19–20 NIV)

Praise be to the LORD, who has given rest to his people Israel just as he promised. Not one word has failed of all the good promises he gave through his servant Moses. (1 Kings 8:56 NIV)

If you make the Most High your dwelling—
even the LORD, who is my refuge—
then no harm will befall you,
no disaster will come near your tent . . .
"Because he loves me," says the LORD, "I will rescue him;
I will protect him, for he acknowledges my name.
He will call upon me, and I will answer him;
I will be with him in trouble,
I will deliver him and honor him.
With long life will I satisfy him and show him my salvation."
(Ps. 91:9–10, 14–16 NIV)

Praise the LORD, O my soul;
all my inmost being, praise his holy name.
Praise the LORD, O my soul,
and forget not all his benefits.

He forgives all my sins
and heals all my diseases;

he redeems my life from the pit and crowns me with love
and compassion.
He satisfies my desires with good things,
so that my youth is renewed like the eagle's. (Ps. 103:1–5 NIV)

Then they cried to the LORD in their trouble,
and he saved them from their distress.
He sent forth his word and healed them;
he rescued them from the grave. (Ps. 107:19-20 NIV)

I will not die but live,
and will proclaim what the LORD has done.
(Ps. 118:17 NIV)

My son, pay attention to what I say;
listen closely to my words.
Do not let them out of your sight,
keep them within your heart;
for they are life to those who find them
and health to a man's whole body.
Above all else, guard your heart,
for it is the wellspring of life. (Prov. 4:20–23 NIV)

So do not fear, for I am with you;
do not be dismayed, for I am your God.
I will strengthen you and help you;
I will uphold you with my righteous right hand.
(Isa. 41:10 NIV)

Surely he took up our infirmities and
carried our sorrows,

yet we considered him stricken by God, smitten by him,
and afflicted.
But he was pierced for our transgressions,
he was crushed for our iniquities;
the punishment that brought us peace was upon him,
and by his wounds we are healed. (Isa. 53:4–5 NIV)

The LORD said . . . "I am watching to see that my word is fulfilled." (Jer. 1:12 NIV)

"But I will restore you to health and heal your wounds," de-
clares the LORD, "because you are called an outcast, Zion for
whom no one cares." (Jer. 30:17 NIV)

Beat your plowshares into swords
And your pruning hooks into spears;
Let the weak say, "I am strong." (Joel 3:10 NKJV)

The Lord will completely destroy the plans that are made
against him. Trouble will not come a second time. (Nah. 1:9
NCV)

A man with leprosy came and knelt before him and said,
"Lord, if you are willing, you can make me clean." Jesus
reached out his hand and touched the man. "I am willing,"
he said. "Be clean!" Immediately he was cured of his leprosy.
(Matt. 8:2–3 NIV)

When evening came, many who were demon-possessed
were brought to him, and he drove out the spirits with a
word and healed all the sick. (Matt. 8:16 NIV)

I tell you the truth, whatever you bind on earth will be bound in heaven, and whatever you loose on earth will be loosed in heaven. Again, I tell you that if two of you on earth agree about anything you ask for, it will be done for you by my Father in heaven. (Matt. 18:18–19 NIV)

Jesus replied, "I tell you the truth, if you have faith and do not doubt . . . you can say to this mountain, 'Go, throw yourself into the sea,' and it will be done." (Matt. 21:21 NIV)

"Have faith in God," Jesus answered. "I tell you the truth, if anyone says to this mountain, 'Go, throw yourself into the sea,' and does not doubt in his heart but believes that what he says will happen, it will be done for him. Therefore I tell you, whatever you ask for in prayer, believe that you have received it, and it will be yours." (Mark 11:22–24 NIV)

He said to them, "Go into all the world and preach the good news to all creation. Whoever believes and is baptized will be saved, but whoever does not believe will be condemned. And these signs will accompany those who believe: In my name they will drive out demons; they will speak in new tongues; they will pick up snakes with their hands; and when they drink deadly poison, it will not hurt them at all; they will place their hands on sick people, and they will get well." (Mark 16:15–18 NIV)

Therefore, the promise comes by faith, so that it may be by grace and may be guaranteed to all Abraham's off-spring—not only to those who are of the law but also to those who are of the faith of Abraham. He is the father of us all. As it is written: "I have made you a father of many nations." He is our father in the sight of God, in whom he believed—the God who gives life to the dead and calls things that are not as though they were. Against all hope, Abraham in hope believed and so became the father of many nations, just as it had been said to him, "So shall your offspring be." Without weakening in his faith, he faced the fact that his body was as good as dead—since he was about a hundred years old—and that Sarah's womb was also dead. Yet he did not waver through unbelief regarding the promise of God, but was strengthened in his faith and gave glory to God, being fully persuaded that God had power to do what he had promised. (Rom. 4:16–21 NIV)

He himself bore our sins in his body on the tree, so that we might die to sins and live for righteousness; by his wounds you have been healed. (1 Peter 2:24 NIV)

Dear friends, if our hearts do not condemn us, we have confidence before God and receive from him anything we ask, because we obey his commands and do what pleases him. (1 John 3:21–22 NIV)

This is the confidence we have in approaching God: that if we ask anything according to his will, he hears us. And if we know that he hears us—whatever we ask—we know that we have what we asked of him. (1 John 5:14–15 NIV)

Dear friend, I pray that you may enjoy good health and that all may go well with you, even as your soul is getting along well. (3 John 2 NIV)

They overcame him by the blood of the Lamb
and by the word of their testimony;
they did not love their lives so much as to shrink
from death. (Rev. 12:11 NIV)

NOTES

Introduction

1. Richard J. Foster, *Prayer: Finding the Heart's True Home* (San Francisco: HarperSanFrancisco, 1992), 216.

Chapter 1

1. Larry Dossey, *Healing Words: The Power of Prayer and the Practice of Medicine* (San Francisco: HarperSanFrancisco, 1993), 90.

2. Carol Osman Brown, "Pathfinder: Prayer in Healing," *HealthLinks* (Fall 1995).

3. Larry Dossey, *Healing Words*, 170.

4. Charles Colson with Ellen Santilli Vaughn, *The Body: Being Light in Darkness* (Dallas: Word, 1992), 335–36.

5. Larry Dossey, *Healing Words*, 37–38.

6. Ibid., 38.

7. "The Ministry of Medicine in the Care of the Whole Person," *Whole-Person Medicine: An International Symposium*, ed. David E. Allen, Lewis Bird, and Robert Herrman (Downer's Grove, IL: InterVarsity Press, 1980), 231.

8. Richard J. Foster, *Prayer: Finding the Heart's True Home* (San Francisco: HarperSanFrancisco, 1992), 204.

9. Jan Ziegler, "Spirituality Returns to the Fold in Medical Practice," *Journal of the National Cancer Institute* 90, no. 17 (2 September 1998), 1255.

10. Burton Goldberg, "Exploring the Body-Mind Connection," *Alternative Medicine: The Definitive Guide* (Future Medical Publishing, Inc.).

11. Larry Dossey, *Healing Words*, 41–42.

12. Harold George Koenig, Mona Smiley, and Jo Ann Ploch Gonzales, *Religion, Health, and Aging: A Review and Theoretical Integration* (New York: Greenwood Press, 1988), Foreword.

13. Carl Jung, *Modern Man in Search of Soul* (New York: Harcourt Brace Jovanovich, 1933), 229.

14. As cited in Jim Ritter, "Med Schools See the Spiritual Side," *Chicago Sun-Times*, 28 September 1997, 37.

15. As cited in "Rx: Religion," *Ladies Home Journal*, December 1997.

16. Mark Moran, "What Is the Role of Spirituality in Medicine?", *American Medical News* 42, no. 14 (12 April 1999), 29.

17. E. Bagiella, T. Powell, and R. P. Sloan, "Religion, Spirituality, and Medicine," *The Lancet* 353, no. 9153 (20 February 1999), 664.

18. Larry Dossey, "Prayer, Exploring Our Power to Heal and Harm," interview by Sheila Walker.

19. "Rx: Religion."

20. "Prayer Affects Your Health," *Restoration News*.

21. Larry Dossey, *Healing Words*, xv.

22. Gary Thomas, "Doctors Who Pray, Part 1," *Christianity Today*, 6 January 1997, 20.

23. Randolph C. Byrd, "Positive Therapeutic Effects of Intercessory Prayer in a Coronary Care Unit Population," *Southern Medical Journal* (July 1988), 826–29.

24. Larry Dossey, *Healing Words*, 186.

25. Howard Wobnsky, "Prayers Do Aid Sick, Study Finds," *Chicago Sun-Times* (26 January 1986), 30.

26. Mike Mitka, "Getting Religion Seen as Help in Being Well," *Journal of the American Medical Association* 280 no. 22, (9 December 1998), 1896–97.

27. Jan Ziegler, "Spirituality Returns to the Fold in Medical Practice," *Journal of the National Cancer Institute* 90, no. 17 (2 September 1998), 1255–57.

28. John H. Christy, "Prayer as Medicine," *Forbes* (23 March 1998).

29. Ibid.

30. Mark Moran, "What Is the Role of Spirituality in Medicine?", *American Medical News* 42, no. 14 (12 April 1999), 29.

31. Jan Ziegler, "Spirituality Returns to the Fold," 1255–57.

32. Bob Pulley, "Putting Prayer to the Test," *Jacksonville Times-Union*, 30 January 1998.

33. Gary Thomas, "Doctors Who Pray, Part 1," 20.

34. Mark Moran, "What Is the Role of Spirituality in Medicine?", 29.

35. Richard Foster, *Prayer, Finding the Heart's True Home* (San Francisco: HarperSanFrancisco, 1992), 204.

36. "Is Faith Enough?", Ivanhoe Broadcast News, Inc.

Chapter 2

1. James S. Gordon, "Combining Modern Science and Natural Healing," lecture presented as part of a Smithsonian Associates Lecture Series, Washington, D.C. (February/March 1999).

2. Pierre L. LeBars, "Ginkgo Biloba Can Stabilize and Even Improve Dementia," *AMA Health Insight.*

3. Alzheimer's Disease and Related Disorders Association, "Ginkgo May Help Alzheimer's," Hometown Pharmacies.

4. R. Doll and R. Peto, "The Causes of Cancer: Quantitative Estimates of Avoidable Risks of Cancer in the United States Today," Oxford University Press, 1981; M. Kurihara et al., "Cancer Mortality Statistics in the World, 1950–1985." University of Nagoya Press, 1989; E. Silverberg and J. A. Lubera, Cancer Statistics, 1988. "CA-A Cancer Journal for Clinicians," 38: 5–22 (1988) (cited in L. Tomatis, ed., "Cancer Causes, Occurrence and Control," Lyon, IARC, 1990).

5. Larry C. Clark, "Selenium and Cancer, "*Journal of the American Medical Association*, Wellness Web.

6. Larry C. Clark, "Selenium Lowers Incidence of Lung, Colorectal, and Prostate Cancer," *Journal of the National Cancer Institute.*

7. Ollie P. Heinonem, "Study in Finland Suggests Vitamin E Prevents Prostate Cancer," *Journal of the National Cancer Institute.*

8. Merrit McKinney, "Vitamin E May Protect Men from Prostate Cancer," *Medical Tribune* (1998).

9. "Garlic and Cancer," Diet & Nutrition Resource Center—Ask the Mayo Dietitian, *Health Oasis Mayo Clinic* (16 October 1996).

10. Dr. Joel Wallach, "Chromium," *Dead Doctors Don't Lie*, 18 May 1999.

11. A. H. Wong, M. Smith, and H. S. Boon, "Herbal Remedies in Psychiatric Practice," Archives of General Psychiatry 55 (11), 1033–44 (November 1998), 99034382.

12. "The Mediterranean Diet, What's the Scoop?", *Healthy Living.*

13. "New Evidence That a Mediterranean Diet Protects Against Heart Disease," *Mediterraneo,* Vol. III, no. 3, March 1999.

Chapter 3

1. S. I. McMillen, *None of These Diseases* (Westwood, NJ: Fleming H. Revell, 1963), cover.

2. "A French Paradox: The Mediterranean Diet," *Ambassade de France en Suede Service Scientifique et Technology,* (www.algonet.se/~frascien).

3. *Circulation: Journal of the American Heart Association,* (99:733-735, 1999) 779–85. Quoted by Center for Cardiovascular Education, Inc., New Providence, NJ.

Chapter 4

1. Malcolm Boyd, *Are You Running With Me, Jesus?* (New York: Avon Books, 1967), 13.

2. Oral Roberts, "Oral Roberts Answers Questions About . . . PRAYER" (Tulsa, OK: Oral Roberts Evangelistic Association, Inc., 1970), 3–4.

3. Joseph L. Gardner, ed., *Atlas of the Bible* (Pleasantville, NY: Reader's Digest Association, 1981), 35.

4. Randolph C. Byrd, "Positive Therapeutic Effects of Intercessory Prayer in a Coronary Care Unit Population," *Southern Medical Journal* (July 1988), 826, quoting C. D. Spivak, "Hebrew Prayers for the Sick," *Annals of Medical History* (Vol. 1, 1917), 83–85.

5. Ibid., 829.

6. Reginald Cherry, *The Bible Cure* (Orlando, FL: Creation House, 1998), 29.

7. Richard J. Foster, *Prayer: Finding the Heart's True Home* (San Francisco: HarperSanFrancisco, 1992).

8. Reginald Cherry, *The Bible Cure*, 46.

9. Bengt R. Hoffman, *Luther and the Mystics* (Minneapolis: Augsburg, 1976), 196.

10. Oral Roberts, "Oral Roberts Answers Questions About . . . PRAYER," 9.

Chapter 6

1. *Whole-Person Medicine: An International Symposium*, ed. Allen, Bird, Herrman, (Downer's Grove, IL: InterVarsity Press, 1980), 49.

2. Reginald Cherry, *The Bible Cure* (Orlando, FL: Creation House, 1998), 49,

3. Reginald Cherry, *The Doctor and the Word* (Orlando, FL: Creation House, 1996), 49.

STUDY AND DISCUSSION GUIDE

Introduction

1. In an age of state-of-the-art technical equipment and "miracle" drugs, there seem to be more people suffering from sickness and disease than ever before. Why do you think this is? How do you explain our society's failure to be cured and get healthier?

2. How do you feel about the obvious increase in "alternative" treatments and therapies outside of conventional medicine, such as the use of so-called psychics, crystals, magnets, aromatherapies, patent medicines, vitamins, minerals, herbs, supplements, and so on?

3. In your experience, do medical doctors and hospital staffs recognize the validity and importance of spiritual faith and prayer in the healing process? Explain. Does your physician pray with you? How would you feel if your physician prayed with you?

4. Do you regularly pray for the healing and recovery of yourself or others in times of illness? What would it take to make you comfortable in petitioning God, specifically and in detail, for healing?

Chapter 1: The Supernatural Connection

1. Do you believe there is a "higher power" that controls or influences the events and circumstances of our lives? Does God really get involved in such things as the provision, prosperity, and health of individual human beings? Explain.

2. What is prayer to you? Does it work? Does it really change "things"? If you do not believe prayer gets results, why do you think it is in universal use?

3. Do you agree with Charles Colson's suggestion that America is a "post Christian culture"? Why? In your experience, is there more or less interest today in the supernatural?

4. Describe a time when you have experienced or observed a division between the spiritual and physical aspects of people in modern medical care—with the physical side being given the primary emphasis. Do you believe this has had any effect on the overall well-being of patients?

5. Based on two hundred medical studies dating back to the nineteenth century, prominent medical researcher Jeff Levin concluded that "religious commitment enhances health and prayer plays a therapeutic role in disease." He also said, "A lack of spirituality seems to be a risk factor for higher rates of illness." How could such convincing proof have been ignored for so long? Do today's doctors and patients believe and act upon this information?

6. In your opinion, why would frequent churchgoers have fewer medical problems, less hospitalizations, and greater

longevity than non-church attenders, as scientific studies have shown?

7. What steps could patients take to help promote more widespread acceptance and practice of "complementary medicine," combining prayer and traditional medicine?

Chapter 2: Complementary Healing Sources: The Natural Side

1. What responsibility does each individual have to pursue all avenues of healing—conventional medical treatment, prayer and spiritual support, and possibly various herbs, vitamins, supplements, and other natural substances? How would you interpret and apply Proverbs 18:9: "He who does not use his endeavors to heal himself is brother to him who commits suicide" (AMPLIFIED)?

2. Dr. Cherry says it is his belief that all healing comes from God, and thus is supernatural. However, he feels that each person has a unique "pathway to healing" that may involve supernatural means, natural means, or a combination of healing treatments and sources. What has been your personal experience? Do you have a family member or friend who has followed a different "pathway to healing"? If so, describe that person's experience.

3. To what do you attribute the phenomenal increase in the sales of vitamins, food supplements, herbs, and other "natural" substances?

4. Historically, new drugs are approved for use in this country only after exhaustive tests and studies, which can cost

tens of millions of dollars and take many years. Physicians are often reluctant to recommend or use nonprescription phytochemicals, herbs, and other substances because "they haven't been studied enough." Yet the World Health Organization has declared that "historical use of an herbal is a valid form of safety and efficacy in the absence of scientific evidence to the contrary."

Do you have concerns about the safety and effectiveness of nonprescription medications? Where could you seek reliable information about natural substances that have proven beneficial effects?

5. Would you be willing to do "something simple" to help protect your body from maladies such as anxiety, depression, arthritis, Alzheimer's disease, cancer, diabetes, heart failure, and cardiovascular artery disease?

There is a growing body of evidence for the benefits of natural substances such as ginkgo biloba, vitamin E, plant-derived estrogens containing isoflavones, selenium, beta-carotene, lycopene (from tomatoes, watermelons, and grapefruits), garlic, *nicotinamide adenine dinucleotide* (NADH), chromium, vanadium, St. John's Wort, valerian, kava kava, saw palmetto, pygeum, coenzyme Q-10, glucosamine sulfate, chondroitin sulfate, and so on.

Simply by determining which products provide benefits or protection for your body's unique needs, then taking a few pills or capsules daily, you possibly could enhance your quality of life, avoid much suffering, and actually lengthen your life. Don't be reluctant to ask your doctor for information and advice. How do you feel about exploring this information?

6. How important is what you eat to your overall health? Six of the ten leading causes of death in this country are directly linked to our nutritional intake, including killers like cardiovascular disease (heart disease and stroke), cancer, lung disease, pneumonia, and diabetes. Immediately after God entered a healing covenant with man in Exodus 15:26, He began describing what man was to eat.

The nutritional and health laws of the Bible are embodied in what is known as the Mediterranean diet, which not only provides protection from cancer and heart diseases, but also has proved to be an excellent program of weight loss and control. This is a healthy, balanced, healing food program that can and should become a part of your lifestyle. To what degree are you willing to consider adopting this diet as a way of eating to live?

Chapter 3: What the Bible Says About Health

1. Dr. Cherry notes that the Holy Scriptures deal with man as a whole person—body, mind, and spirit—nurturing, protecting, and guiding human beings to achieve their full potential in every area of their being. What examples of beneficial biblical advice can you cite? (For example, dietary laws, personal hygiene, bodily rest, sexual conduct, crop rotation, financial management, and so on.)

2. What are the consequences of ignoring or deliberately breaking God's laws? How do you interpret Proverbs 26:2: "The curse causeless shall not come" (KJV)?

3. Two key "thou shalt nots" in God's health plan are don't *eat* fat and don't *be* fat (see Lev. 3:17 NIV and Luke 21:34

AMPLIFIED). Why do you think modern man has felt he could ignore these laws with impunity? Could these failures contribute to the prevalence of health problems in our society?

4. The Bible provides a dramatic case study of God's health food plan tested against a Babylonian diet of wine and "rich dainties" (Dan. 1). What did Daniel, Shadrach, Meshach, and Abednego eat? How did their physical condition and mental alertness compare to the Babylonian "control group" at the end of the test period? What does this suggest about your diet?

5. What does Dr. Cherry mean when he says that science is "walking in the footsteps of God" and is still in the position of "catching up" with the ancient laws God gave His people thirty-five centuries ago in the Bible?

Chapter 4: Do You Know How to Pray?
1. What are the six principles of praying Jesus taught His disciples—and us—in the Lord's Prayer?

2. Dr. Cherry cited faith and scientific evidence as two reasons he accepts God's Word as trustworthy. What are your reasons for believing in and trusting the truths and teachings of the Bible?

3. "Who has not, during a time of illness or pain, cried out to a higher being for help and healing?" What about you? What's your story? Did God heal and respond to your cry? How did you know God heard your prayer? Did you receive the answer you needed and expected?

4. What are the "rules" or guidelines for prayer that Dr. Cherry describes?

5. How many of the different kinds of prayer listed are you familiar with? Which are the most meaningful and important to you? What kind of prayer do you use most often?

6. If faith is essential to getting our prayers answered, where do we get faith? Will God ask for what is beyond our ability?

7. How can we know God's will for our lives? Are there some things we don't even need to seek His will about—such as lying, stealing, killing, or committing adultery? What about healing?

8. What are we supposed to pray about? How are we to pray? Are we "bothering" God when we share our concerns, anxieties, worries, needs, and requests?

Chapter 5: A Doctor Learns How to Pray
for the Sick

1. Dr. Cherry relates that he became angry and bitter toward God when a college professor declared that "sickness and disease are tools God uses to teach people lessons. God sends pain and suffering to turn people back to the Lord, or to teach them to trust and depend on God." Have you been disturbed by hearing this or other nonbiblical assertions? What other commonly heard but unscriptural teachings have you encountered?

2. Why do we sometimes use "tunnel vision," focusing on specific characteristics of individuals rather than seeing the whole person?

3. Dr. Cherry says that at first he tried to measure success by money, recognition, power, and prestige. But he wasn't satisfied or fulfilled. How do you measure success—in your career, your relationships, with your family, and in your spiritual life?

4. One person living the Christian life had a profound impact on Dr. Cherry and made him aware of his need for God. Who or what was the most effective witness in your life? How has God used you to reach someone else with the gospel?

5. Has your medical treatment in the past focused only on "the part that hurts" rather than a personalized, comprehensive pathway to healing? Are you willing to allow God to direct you in formulating a healthful lifestyle that combines a proper diet, preventive health care, exercise, a balanced program of vitamins, herbs, minerals, supplements, and other natural substances, along with spiritual fortification?

Chapter 6: The Six Biblical Foundations for Healing

1. F. F. Bosworth said, "Instead of saying, 'Pray for me,' many people should first say, 'Teach me God's Word, so that I can intelligently co-operate with God for my recovery.'" What did Bosworth mean by this? Do you think that a person who

ignores the Bible's counsel on health and fails to take care of his physical body is more likely or less likely to receive supernatural healing?

2. Do you believe that God wants you (and everyone) to be healed? What convinces you?

3. What does Dr. Cherry mean when he says that if we believe in salvation, we must also believe in healing? Are you convinced that Christ's sacrifice paid for and provided a double cure for man's double curse?

4. How many biblical examples can you think of that illustrate the necessity and value of persistence and perseverance? How long does your faith last when you are praying for healing? Resolve to practice determination—never give up.

5. Dr. Cherry suggests that a "feisty" attitude—the opposite of passivity—is a foundation for healing. This requires keeping our imagination in check and guarding our thoughts and our words. He also advises us to speak life! If you don't know what to say, speak God's Word! Pick out three of your favorite faith-building Bible promises and say them aloud, putting your name into the verses where possible. Do it with an air of authority and "lively aggressiveness."

6. God has a pathway of healing for you. It is His plan and His will for you. Are you willing to set aside your expectations and surrender to God's way? Read Jeremiah 29:13 (KJV) and consider how it applies to your finding the pathway to healing God has prepared for you.

7. All healing comes from God, and He may use both natural and supernatural means to deliver it to us. Dr. Cherry believes that, as a general rule, God asks us to do what we can do in the natural as He acts in our behalf in the supernatural. Has this been true in your experience?

Chapter 7: God Still Heals Today

1. Face up to Dr. Cherry's challenge at the beginning of Chapter 7. Are you being diligent in the proper care of your body? If you don't do the things you know to do in the natural, how long will it take for your body to break down again even if you are healed of your current affliction?

2. Practice the concept of "speaking to your mountain" from Mark 11:23. Don't pray in general—be specific in addressing your condition and your symptoms and telling them where to go. Visualize and describe the normal working of your physical body and pray for perfection. Don't doubt—believe that the things you say will come to pass.

3. Do you think that being given more complete information about ulcerative colitis helped Frank Wilson be more positive and effective in praying for his healing? Do you have the information you need from your doctor to "speak to your mountain"?

4. Were Charles Cunningham's symptoms "real" even though there was nothing physically wrong with him? Read 1 John 4:18 (KJV)—"Fear hath torment." What is the best treatment for fear and worry?

180

Chapter 8: The Most Important Prayer
You'll Ever Pray

1. How could finding forgiveness of sin and freedom from guilt through Jesus Christ have a positive impact on a person's physical health and well-being?

2. What are the four scriptural stepping-stones to a new life in Christ? Find these in the chapter text. Mark the verses in your Bible.

3. Express in your own words your understanding of what it means to be "born again" (see John 3:5–6 NIV).

4. Have you prayed the sinner's prayer? If not, why not do it right now? If so, welcome to the family of God!

5. Once you have accepted Christ as your Lord and Savior, here's what's next:

A. Talk to God—simply and directly, as a child talks to his father. Take time to listen for His voice speaking to you. This is prayer. Do it often.

B. Read the Bible. The Holy Spirit will help you understand it. Start with John's Gospel, and then move to the Psalms and Proverbs. Read some every day.

C. Find a good church that will teach you and help you grow spiritually. Make some Christian friends and spend some time with them. Enjoy your new life.

The Healing Word

1. Read the Scripture verses about healing in this chapter often. Read them aloud and listen to what God's voice is saying. If you need healing, read the verses daily.

2. Look up each verse in your favorite modern translation of the Bible. Sometimes a different version emphasizes the unchanging truth of God's Word in a different way that is especially meaningful.

3. Pick out your five favorite verses. Memorize them and quote them several times a day.

ABOUT THE AUTHOR

Reginald Cherry, M.D., attended Baylor University and the University of Texas Medical School. He formerly practiced medicine with Dr. Kenneth Cooper, who introduced him to the concepts of preventive medicine.

Dr. Cherry owns and operates the R. B. Cherry Clinic in Houston, Texas, which is noted for its unique approach to medicine, including the practice of traditional medicine, alternative medicine, and praying for the sick.

He and his wife, Linda, are hosts of *The Doctor and the Word*, TBN's number one rated television show. He is the author of the best-sellers *The Doctor and the Word* and *The Bible Cure*.